THE 100 GREATEST COMMODORE 64 GAMES

Tom Crossland

Contents

AUTHOR'S NOTE

The first C64 game I ever played was 1983's Falcon Patrol by Steve Lee. I suspect this game might have come free with the computer. Falcon Patrol is a side on shoot em up. The player plays the pilot of a jet fighter in the Falcon Patrol squadron. Other jets have to be battled and prevented from bombing the airfields. The player has to use the airfields to refuel and also be resupplied with ammunition. The player in Falcon Patrol has three jets - another is given every 3000 points. Falcon Patrol is a very basic side on scrolling shooter. It has fairly spartan graphics, the scrolling is a trifle jittery, and sometimes the missiles go right through planes without exploding. But to me Falcon Patrol was extremely addictive and very atmospheric. It was very special. The sound effects - especially the refuelling sound – add greatly to the game. Falcon Patrol was my gateway to an incredible range of games right through the peak golden years of the C64.

The list of games that follows is of course subjective and reflects my own personal tastes. Nonetheless, there is still a remarkably diverse and eclectic range of games in this book. You might disagree with a few inclusions (and exclusions!) but that's all part of the fun of lists. One could easily come up with a list of more than one hundred great C64 games because there were thousands of games produced for this machine and many of them were fantastic. By way of example, I could find no room in this list for games like Thrust, Bangkok Knights, Ballblazer, Fight Night, Exile, Curse of the Azure Bonds, and Pole Position. There are simply too many good games on the C64 to include everything.

The C64 did of course have its share of clunkers and terrible games but - happily - we don't have to worry too much about them. This book is about good games. Not just good games but classics of their era. The Commodore 64 was an incredible piece of tech for its time and left a generation with enough happy and nostalgic gaming memories to last a lifetime.

Though these games often seem primitive now from a modern vantage point (as we battle our way through the likes of Doom Eternal) this was anything but the case in the 1980s. C64 kids from that decade will never forget pounding those planes with anti-aircraft fire in Beach Head or the digitised cry of anguish in Impossible Mission when you mistimed a jump and fell into what seemed like infinity. Even little games that seemed throwaway and simple like Hunchback II are ingrained in my memories forever.

The C64 was eventually even able to more or less (with a few miss-steps along the way) replicate the arcade experience for home gamers - which might not sound like much today but in the 1980s was a very big deal. To be able to play faithful versions of things like Ghosts n' Goblins and Kung Fu Master in your home was a novelty indeed in the mid eighties. It was like having an arcade machine in your living room. Best of all, once you'd shelled out for the game, you didn't have to put any coins in to play it!

As far as the C64 went, the games to approach with some degree of caution were the licenced games. Companies would get the rights to some popular movie or television show like Knight Rider and inevitably the game they knocked up with said licence would be terrible. That cover art would always lure you in though. Though it's far from the worst game ever made one of my least favourite licenced experiences was Airwolf. A game based on Airwolf! Eighties kids like me couldn't wait to get home and experience some high-tech helicopter action for themselves. What they got instead was a game where Airwolf is trapped in a cave system! Fiddly, frustrating, and nigh on impossible, Airwolf definitely wasn't something I was in a rush to go back to. I remember being dreadfully disappointed too by a game based on Judge Dredd.

Not all the licenced games on the C64 were terrible though. There were some gems hidden amongst them if one was willing to sift through the dross (naturally, Commodore User and ZZAP!64 were invaluable for research before you parted with any of your parents' hard earned money). There are a decent smattering of licenced games in the book which follows. A forgotten classic based on Alien for example and even a fascinating game based on a controversial Liverpudlian pop group.

A common tactic with games companies was to get a celebrity sportsman to endorse their game. So you'd get things like Frank Bruno's Boxing or Alex Higgins World Snooker. These sporting endorsements did not always guarantee a great game but there were definitely some classics. Barry McGuigan's Boxing and Emlyn Hughes Football are two notable examples of the good games in this specific genre. One of the most famous early C64 games was Daley Thompson's Decathlon. Though it didn't make this book I remember the game as being sort of fun but infamous for the dreaded 'joystick waggling' mechanic. To make Daley run faster in the game you had to waggle the joystick from side to side as rapidly as you could. Games like this must have destroyed a fair few joysticks.

Another notorious 'joystick waggler' was Hyper Sports (which is a much better game than Daley Thompson's Decathlon and DOES make it into this book). Years and decades later, I was playing FEAR 2 and encountered a moment in the game where you have to frenziedly stab at the mouse button to have a hand to hand strangling fight with a villain. Talk about Daley Thompson's Decathlon flashbacks! I really hope that mouse mechanic doesn't catch on again.

The golden age of the C64 was the mid 1980s. The machine endured for much longer than that but in the end many people upgraded to the Amiga (which was also fantastic but sadly doomed) or drifted away to other machines. Are C64 games still worth playing today - even if you have all the latest modern releases? My answer to that question is yes! Commodore C64 games are still fun and still worth exploring. Games like Summer Games II, Leader Board and Boulder Dash are still a pleasure to dig out and play.

And there are plenty of other classics too, as we shall see in the book that follows. Shooting games, strategy games, arcade adventures, space flight simulators, sports simulations, racing games, fantasy games, horror games, combat games, boxing games, platform games, and so on. So, without any further delay, let us begin our countdown (in alphabetical order of course) of the one hundred greatest C64 games. Let the nostalgia commence...

THE 100 GREATEST COMMODORE 64 GAMES

ALIEN (1984)

Label: Argus Press Software, Designer: Paul Clansey

Alien is an adventure/strategy game based on the classic 1979 film by Ridley Scott. Though it might appear simple on the surface this is a surprisingly sophisticated game that was way ahead of its time. The music is famously creepy (that opening theme is both jaunty and sinister to remarkable effect) and one might argue that purely in terms of atmosphere and tone this is one of the most faithful of the many games based on the Alien franchise. The game features all the characters from the film and takes place just after the alien has hatched and broken loose on your ship the Nostromo. The look of the game is a top down view of the layout of the ship. Using commands you move the characters around with the aim of killing the alien.

There are various ways you can kill the alien - like trapping the creature and blasting it out of an airlock. You have a number of tasks to achieve (capturing Jones the cat is rather pesky) and you have the added trouble of not knowing which one of the crew is the duplicitous android working for the sinister company in charge of the ship. The identity of the android changes with each new game just to make sure you never know who the traitor is. The android will attempt to sabotage the player's strategy to defeat the alien. Each time the game starts one of the crew is randomly killed by playing host to the creature. It's nice that the game subverts your knowledge of the film to keep you guessing. By the way, I love the box with this game. It looks like a mini VHS case and has a nice booklet with photographs of all the characters from the film.

The first part of the game is quite slow and gives you a chance to get hold of enough weapons for your characters so they can fight back against the acid blooded xenomorph.

The tension amps up once the alien enters the fray and it is genuinely spooky and scary when the game informs you that one of the characters is under attack. When this happens a graphic of the alien fills up the screen. You could argue that this game is actually the grandfather of the survival horror genre. The AI in the game is impressive for the era (characters might refuse a command if they are nervous or feel under threat) and no two games of this are the same. This is a fascinating and complex early C64 strategy game and fairly unique. There's nothing quite like it really.

The flaws in the game are the garish green screens which map out the Nostromo and also the fact that dispensing commands can be cumbersome and not exactly swift - which obviously doesn't help if you need to do something quickly! This game won't be everyone's cup of tea but it deserves a small cloud in C64 heaven. If you like strategy games and are a fan of the Alien franchise this can be a rewarding experience. Though the games don't last long it is very difficult to kill the alien - which does at least give the game more playability and make it more of a challenge.

Alien is sort of game that will divide opinion (I suspect a lot of kids in 1984 probably loaded this up and couldn't make nor tail out of it and so moved swiftly onto something else) but if you like immersive strategy games and the Alien franchise you should find this an interesting experience. You wouldn't say that Alien was a truly great game but it is an ambitious and clever one and left a big impression on me.

Alien is a game which illustrates how atmosphere is a fundamental part of computer games - especially ones that inhabit the horror genre like this. The fact that this game was was an acquired taste was illustrated by the spread of reviews of received. Some found it a challenging strategy game that would keep you engrossed with weeks and others found it a dull looking game which lacked action. Ultimately, it was all in the eye of the beholder. My own view is that Alien - for all its flaws - is a fascinating and atmospheric game.

ALIENS (1987)

Label: Electric Dreams, Designer: Mark Eyles

Aliens is based on the classic 1986 film sequel Aliens. In the game a remote planet has been colonised by humans. Unfortunately it is also host to dangerous aliens. The survivor of the first encounter with these dangerous alien creatures - Ellen Ripley - leads a team of individuals to go back to the planet and check the human base for survivors. The player controls the team members: Ripley; soldiers Gorman, Hicks and Vasquez; Bishop the android; and corporation representative Burke.

The player in Aliens can see the base through a camera on the team members helmets. The player moves the characters through different rooms in the base. Doors are locked, sealed or blown up. The Aliens move through the base leaving organic material - that creates face hugger creatures which attack and impregnate the team with an alien. Aliens and organic material can be shot and destroyed but ammunition is limited and the player must visit the armoury to be resupplied. Members have an energy bar and have to rest to replenish it. Crew members are sometimes captured by the aliens and must be rescued. The control room - for heating and lighting - must be defended. The aim is to guide Ripley to the Queen's chamber to destroy the Queen Alien.

C64 film tie ins were too often awful with companies simply trying to cash in on a licenced property and throwing out a game as soon as they could. They were usually some awful side scrolling platform game/shoot em up but Aliens is good movie adaption and at least tried something new. The gameplay in Aliens is a good representation of the film's plot. and the graphics are very good, again suiting the style of the film. Unfortunately there is no music for this one though. There are a series of suitably eerie sound effects though - such as the alarm that sounds when an alien is near.

The game is quite tough but fun to play. It is addictive and gets quite tense when crises start to happen. There is a great atmosphere from the film and the aliens are nicely depicted. One might argue that the game becomes a little samey in the end with the lack of variety in the backdrops but this is an interesting attempt at what is essentially a very early sort of first person shooter. C64 owners would have been impressed by the look of Aliens and if you fell for the immersive atmosphere of the game then it was an interesting and even spooky experience. This game is not perfect (and can be frustrating) but you can see that a lot of effort has gone into it.

Another official Aliens game was made (by Activision) in 1986 - the Activision going for a mini-game sort of approach with contrasting levels. The Activision game has some nice illustrations of scenes from the film and begins with a fairly impressive (for the time) sequence where you have to pilot the dropship to the surface of LV426. After this there is a bit too much of moving around corridors with little stick men Colonial Marines. This section of the Activision game is a lot less polished than the Electric Dreams game. There's a very basic shooting section after this and then you take on the Alien Queen in Ripley's power-loader in what is a fairly decent looking last section. The Aliens game by Activision is pretty average on the whole compared to the Electric Dreams one but C64 or Aliens completists should probably check out both games because the second one definitely has its fans too.

ARCHON: THE LIGHT AND THE DARK (1983)

Label: Free Fall Associates, Designer: Jon Freeman, Paul Reiche III

Archon: The Light and the Dark is one of the undisputed early classics of the C64 and a unique game with a genius concept. The concept is basically chess but with an arcade gameplay component. The game plays out on what looks like a chessboard and the goal is to secure five power point squares. When two pieces end up on the same square it doesn't work like chess (where the lower ranking figurine is immediately removed from the game) but instead the two opposing figures are placed within an arcade style combat arena and must fight it out to see who survives and wins the square!

The various pieces you move around in the game all have different strengths and weaknesses so an element of strategy is involved in choosing which piece to go up against another. Some of the figures have special abilities - like the ability to cast spells or shapeshift. This game is basically like chess crossed with Dungeons & Dragons crossed with some vintage arcade action. The concept was highly addictive to C64 gamers in the early eighties and many of them played Archon to death. There's no doubt that this game has a brilliant concept behind it. This is also a really good two player game.

This game was originally written for the Atari and ported to other platforms - including of course the C64. The game's graphics are nothing fancy but because a lot of the game is framed by what looks like a chessboard this gives much of the visual presentation a stylish and fairly timeless feel.

Chessboards just look nice don't they? The arcade fighting sections are where Archon shows its age more readily as these are fairly primitive to modern eyes. However, the arcade sections are fun. The gameplay is fine and because you are battling for power points in the game you are completely absorbed in the combat and not really taking much notice of the graphics anyway.

Archon: The Light and the Dark is a really great game on the whole. In 1984 there was a sequel to this game titled Archon II: Adept. The general consensus is that the sequel is not as good nor as essential as the original. Many felt the second game was too complex although ZZAP!64 complained that it relied too much on joystick waggling arcade action! If you like

the first game you should probably check out Archon II at
some point but the balance between strategy and gameplay
patently wasn't as perfect as in the first game. If you lower
your expectations though you might enjoy it. Don't miss
playing the original classic game though.

ARMALYTE (1988)

*Label: Cyberdyne Systems, Designer: Dan Phillips, John
Kemp*

Armalyte is a horizontally scrolling shooter and a sequel to
Delta (which is also well worth playing). There were many
games of this type on the C64 but Armalyte really stood out
from the pack with its fast paced action and beautiful graphics.
This is definitely a masterpiece of the C64 shoot em up genre.

The aim of the game is (naturally) to reach the end of each
scrolling level. There are eight screens in all and some fiendish
boss battles - just to make sure you get a proper challenge. As
the game progresses you can power up your weapons and get
power upgrades. Best of all you can earn various Super
Weapons which dispense a satisfying amount of damage on
the unfortunate enemies. There is also a two-player mode.

Where this game really scored was in the amount of detail on
the screen. Not just enemy ships (which came in a variety of
guises and designs) but huge obstacles and traps which had to
be blasted at strategic points before one could make progress.
This game is considered to be very difficult so if you find these
types of games too easy at times you could be assured of a
fairly decent challenge here. As far as horizontally scrolling
shooters go there were several that were worthy of a place in
this list and worth playing but I enjoyed Armalyte more than
most for its bright trippy graphics and frenzied boss fights. It's
obviously a matter of personal taste though. If you like these
types of games this is definitely one to take a look at.

What really makes this game memorable is the fact that so much is happening on the screen at any one time. You could certainly never accuse this game of going through the motions. There are bright colours and objects, enemies glow and rotate, and the laser effects from your weapons are satisfying and striking. This is not one of those games either where it becomes easy once you learn the attack patterns of the enemy ships. This game poses a welcome challenge and will engulf you in more and more mayhem the longer you get into it.

Armalyte is a classic arcade style shooter and remains a lot of fun to play. This was one of the most polished shooters of the long and enjoyable C64 era and that's saying something because there were literally hundreds of them. This game earned a coveted Gold Medal award in ZZAP!64 with 98%. It's a game which really pushed the hardware of the C64 and showed what the machine was capable of. There were many games similar to Armalyte on the C64 but few were as polished and playable as this one.

AZTEC CHALLENGE (1983)

Label: COSMI, Creator: Paul Norman

In Aztec Challenge the player is an Aztec warrior obstreperously racing through temples and avoiding various deadly obstacles. The first level is The Gauntlet. The player runs towards a Temple and either side are Aztecs throwing spears - which must be jumped over or ducked under. If the player is hit by a spear they are placed at the start of the level again. Level 2 is The Stairs. The player is climbing up the stairs of the temple and must avoid stone blocks which are being thrown. Level 3 is The Temple. The player must avoid (you guessed it) various booby traps.

Level 4 is The Vermin - the player has to avoid various

creatures like scorpions. Level 5 is Hopaztec in which the player has to cross a tiled floor - some of the tiles are booby trapped. Level 6 is Piranha where the player has to (as the title suggests) swim across a lake avoiding piranha fish. Level 7 is The Bridge - where the player runs over a bridge jumping over holes in the bridge which are different sizes. Yes, it's safe to say that the Aztec warrior you control is in for a very dangerous and pesky time indeed!

Aztec Challenge is something of a cult game. The graphics seem quite basic (crudely so at times) but the animations and scrolling effects are good and there is a nice variety in the levels. This is basically like an amusing spin on those multi-sports games which became a staple of the C64. If nothing else Aztec Challenge scores high marks for originality and it's very addictive and playable too. There are 3D perspectives from behind the player, side on view levels and top down view levels so the levels all seem different. This is one of those early simple and charming C64 arcade games which are extremely addictive.

Aztec Challenge has a great atmosphere with the Aztec setting and mysterious music. Aztec Challenge is quite difficult and unforgiving at times but this helps with the replayability of the game. The designer Paul Norman also made the Forbidden Forest games. He later made a new version of Aztec Challenge called Azteca: Queen of Quetzalcoatl and released it via his website. The original game was for the Atari 8 bit computers and was a complete side scroller without 3D sections.

If you like fast and frenzied (not to mention unusual) sports style games with a twist then Aztec Challenge is a lot of fun. This game is memorable too and not one you'll forget in a hurry. It isn't the best looking game in the world (even for the time it came out) but it has bags of character and atmosphere and the gameplay is engaging and compulsive.

BARBARIAN (1987)

Label: Place Software, Designer: Stanley Schembri

Barbarian is a swords and sandals fighting game. The player is a barbarian who is a highly skilled swordsman. Sorcerer Drax threatens Jewel City with destruction if he does not get his villainous mitts on Jewel City's Princess Mariana. Drax obviously cannot take the Princess if he's defeated in a duel so the barbarian takes him on. In the first part of the game different opponents are taken on in practice. In the second part the Princess must be fought for. Different fighters are taken on - finishing with Drax. There are sixteen fighting moves. Energy is signified by six dots. They go down in half or full amounts depending on strength of hit. A two player game is available.

Barbarian is a fun fighting game. It makes a change also to have a beat em up game outside the usual martial arts setting! The game has a great atmosphere with the fantasy setting. There are some nice touches - such as a gnome taking away a severed head. There are good controls and challenging computer opponents. There's a great music score too. While there were no shortage of fighting games on the C64, Barbarian was inventive and different enough to justify its own existence and is a really solid and enjoyable beat em up in its own right.

The only criticism one might have of Barbarian is that game seems a trifle slow at times. The combat is decent enough though and the backdrops and graphics make the game feel immersive and enjoyable. You could just as well include the 1988 sequel Barbarian II: The Dungeon of Drax in this book too. Barbarian II is graphically even more impressive than the first game with a wider variety of opponents and monsters to fight. The opponents in the sequel tend to have more elaborate (and enjoyably strange) designs and you can see that the game has been given an impressive graphical tweak in comparison to the original.

Barbarian II also has some impressive world-building in the way that it opens up the universe of the game and makes everything feel bigger and bolder. Most critics seem to think that Barbarian II: The Dungeon of Drax was even better than the original. The best thing to do of course is simply play both games! The Barbarian games remain classics of the C64 era and are a lot of fun. C64 gamers who were a trifle bored of pyjama clad kung fu capers with a far east backdrop at least got something fairly new and fresh with Barbarian. The atmosphere and graphics alone make these games memorable.

BARRY McGUIGAN WORLD CHAMPIONSHIP BOXING (1985)

Label: Sportsware Productions, Designer: Troy Lyndon

Barry McGuigan World Championship Boxing is a boxing game named after the Irish boxer and former WBA featherweight champion Barry McGuigan. In this side on simulation, the player controls a boxer who rises up the ratings by winning fights. The player can create a boxer and choose race, hair colour, trunks, image, attitude, stamina, agility, strength, endurance, best punch, and recovery. Each boxer has a different set of abilities - one, for example, might be a big puncher but not have much endurance. The player has to move up the rankings and has a choice of a few boxers at their current level. Before a fight the boxer trains and the different types of training have an effect on the different abilities.

"Light Bag" raises the boxer's speed. "Heavy Bag" on the other hand improves the force of the blows. "Spar Time" shortens the recovery time. "Weights" raises the boxer's strength. "Roadwork" improves the stamina. There are a number of different boxing moves - cross, block, body punch, jab, hook and uppercut. On the screen during the fight is the time of the round, round number, endurance, points in the fight, and count – for when a boxer is knocked down.

Barry McGuigan World Championship Boxing is probably the best boxing game for the C64 and all the more effective for eschewing the cartoonish 'comedy' style of other C64 boxing games. Although the graphics may look very simple, Barry McGuigan World Championship Boxing is very atmospheric and the boxers have real personality. Boxers can be created and the boxers in the game have different attributes. If you don't have much stamina left you have to box smart to try and not get knocked out. The boxing animations are very good. There are a wide range of punches so you can box in different style and the knock-downs are very satisfying.

The game is very playable and the ability to create a boxer gives the game longevity. The game was called Star Rank Boxing in the US. What I love most about Barry McGuigan World Championship Boxing is that it feels like it has more depth than other boxing games. In fights for example you can block punches to good effect and bide your time. This isn't just the usual button mashing all action combat game. It might not be the most eye-catching game visually but Barry McGuigan World Championship Boxing is a well designed and very playable game. This was definitely one of my favourite fighting games on the C64.

Another good boxing game released in 1985 was Accolade's Fight Night. This game is graphically impressive but it doesn't have the depth of satisfying gameplay offered by Barry McGuigan World Championship Boxing and goes for an overtly tongue-in-cheek approach. Fight Night is fun but Barry McGuigan World Championship Boxing was much better. The other famous boxing game on the C64 was Frank Bruno's Boxing - which was released by Elite in 1985. This game is basically a copy of a famous game called Super-Punch Out from other platforms. Frank Bruno's Boxing is quite cartoonish with comedy opponents. The game is perfectly

decent and fun for a while but it was definitely a rung below
Barry McGuigan World Championship Boxing and Fight
Night. Elite definitely got their timing wrong with the release
of Frank Bruno's Boxing because it came out very shortly after
the much superior Barry McGuigan World Championship
Boxing and Fight Night!

BATTLE THROUGH TIME (1984)

Label: Anirog Software, Designer: Ken Grant

Battle Through Time is an action and shoot em up game. It is a
side scrolling game in which the player drives a jeep jumping
over obstacles and potholes attacking enemies in the air and
on the ground. When the player has driven ten miles the next
level is accessed. There are seven levels: World War I, World
War II, The Korean War, The Vietnam War, World War III,
War Mutations (an alien looking landscape) and In the
Beginning - back to Stone Age with a Tyrannosaurus Rex as an
end-of-level boss! If the game is completed it restarts with a
slightly harder difficulty.

This is a fun game with an irresistible time travelling element.
The graphics are very pleasant and atmospheric though of
course rather dated. This is one of those games that doesn't
look much at first glance but then offers bags of gameplay.
Appearances can de deceptive! You don't necessarily have to
have the best looking graphics in the world to create a great
game. Not that Battle Through Time looks bad anywhere. It is
presented in pleasant enough fashion for what it is.

Each level in Battle Through Time has its own music theme
based on famous music such a Symphony #5 by Ludwig van
Beethoven and The Blue Danube by Johann Strauss the
Younger and also contemporary music such as the Darth
Vader theme. The different renditions of famous songs for
each level is a nice touch. It is very mysterious and

atmospheric game with the different time periods and some interesting historical commentary in some of the levels. The difficulty level is about right. This is a good early C64 game and was patently influenced by arcade game Moon Patrol.

Battle Through Time is a very addictive game that becomes very engrossing. You will have to pay attention both to what is above you and ahead of you in this game. Things get very frantic and fun at times. Battle Through Time is an enjoyable little classic from the early years of the C64. The game is inventive, entertaining, and has plenty of character. Though it may not look like the most ambitious game in the world at first in terms of its visual presentation the scrolling and mountain backdrops are all nicely done and enjoyable.

A game worth a look if you enjoyed Battle Through Time is the 1988 Hewson release Battle Valley. In this detailed and attractive looking two-way horizontal shooter you can control a helicopter or a jeep as you battle terrorists and complete objectives in a variety of backdrops. Battle Valley is clearly inspired by games like Battle Through Time but is good enough to be a satisfying game in its own right and not merely a clone of anything in particular. The parallax scrolling in the game is excellent. Best of all, Battle Valley was a budget release so only cost a few quid to buy at the time.

BEACH HEAD (1983)

Label: Access Software, Designer: Bruce Carver

Beach Head is a military action game set in the Pacific Theatre of World War 2. An island has been seized and you have to take it back. Those who were around for the early years of the C64 will probably have fond nostalgic memories of playing this game. Beach Head is definitely one of those games that lodges in the memory. The game has various levels and the main objective is to stop the enemy from breaking through. The most memorable level has you controlling anti-aircraft guns and trying to destroy enemy planes as they make their way towards your position. You have to time your shots and anticipate when the plane will enter the line of fire. The sound effects of the planes and bombs are very nicely done in this section and add to the all action aura of the game.

Though it might not look much to today's gamers this was pretty amazing stuff in 1983 to be part of a big navel battle with ships dotting the horizon and planes growing steadily larger as they loom into view and prepare to attack. The climax has you destroying a huge gun emplacement and there's quite a good (if slightly fiddly) tank section too. Though quite primitive in places by today's standards the game (especially the naval section) is very good for the era and generally very playable. I gather some gaming critics at the time felt the game was a little too easy but this is one of the few minor quibbles one could throw in the direction of Beach Head. If you owned a C64 in the 1980s you almost certainly would have played this game at some point and you most likely had a lot of fun.

In 1996, Computer Gaming World named Beach Head the 117th-best computer game ever released. Beach Head might seem rather simplistic today but it was pretty amazing for 1983. It's a fun game that is easy to play and get into. There was something about Beach Head that made you return to the game again and again. In 1983 Beach Head was an amazing experience for young C64 kids. I'll never forgot that early section where you have a guide a ship to sea and avoid torpedoes. This section seems preposterously primitive today in terms of graphics but guiding that ship out was always amazingly satisfying to do.

There was a sequel to Beach Head in 1985 titled Beach-Head II: The Dictator Strikes Back. This game is equally as good as the original and offers four levels composed of mini-games. The levels are different enough to give the game some welcome variety. What people remember most about the sequel is that it had synthesized speech - so you'd hear characters in the game shout things like "Hey! Don't shoot me", "Medic!" and "You can't hurt me!".

The sequel has a rail shooter type section, a helicopter section (which plays like one of those 1942 style games) and an enjoyable climax where you throw knives at the villain from the other side of a river (the Dictator is naturally throwing knives back too). Though you don't get many levels (which is a shame) Beach-Head II: The Dictator Strikes Back is very playable and inventive and a satisfyingly solid sequel. The most important thing about the sequel is that it feels different - which still retaining plenty of Beach Head DNA and residue. Happily, you don't feel as if you are simply getting the same game again.

I would certainly recommend both of the Beach Head games and although they aren't perfect they are both classic C64 fun. The two games are inventive and entertaining. You do wish they had been a bit longer though. A few more levels would have been very welcome and given them even more playability.

BLUE MAX (1983)

Label: US Gold, Designer: Stephen C. Biggs

Blue Max is one of those games that all C64 users must have played at some point or other. Blue Max is a shoot em up game. The player pilots a Sopwith Camel biplane during World War 1. The player can use machine gun and bombs to destroy other planes and buildings on the ground. There are three areas with targets to destroy. The game was originally written for the Atari 8 bit systems and was inspired by River Raid and the arcade shooter Zaxxon (which also had the same distinctive slanting layout as Blue Max).

Blue Max is a great shoot em up and very playable. The diagonal angle makes a change from the top down and side on shooters. Also the World War 1 setting makes a change from the futuristic setting of other shooters. Blue Max is strangely addictive and pretty good fun as far as these types of games go. It scores highly on atmosphere and the diagonal gameplay makes it oddly entrancing and addictive. There are some nice touches in this game - like the ability to fly under bridges. This is undoubtedly one of those sturdy early classics of the C64 years and a great little shooting game.

In 1984 there was a sequel titled Blue Max 2001. As the name suggests, this was a futuristic rather than a historical shooting game. I'm not quite sure how they managed to bungle the Blue Max formula (a simple but winning formula you might think) with the sequel as Blue Max 2001 is pretty poor to be honest and a very pale imitation of the first game. What really sinks the sequel in the end is the frustratingly unresponsive and awkward control system. It's a shame the second game is so forgettable as the original is a justly famous C64 classic.

If you like the style of game offered by Blue Max you should consider playing the 1986 Mastertronic game Panther - which was created by the same person as Blue Max. Panther is a diagonally scrolling isometric shoot em up game. Phlegms from Bo Gee have invaded Earth. They have destroyed the city of Xenon. But humans are still hiding in bunkers - including important military personnel. They need to be rescued. The player controls a Panther space craft and has to shoot alien ships and rescue the humans. A simple fun shoot em up, Panther which was a budget title from Mastertronic when released so great value for money. It has a wonderful epic soundtrack. There are good controls and creepy atmospheric graphics and alien enemies. The isometric scrolling in Panther is very smooth and there is a lot of fun shoot em up action. The controls are easy to use and very responsive.

If you like Blue Max and Panther you will almost certainly have played Zaxxon - which was released on the C64 by Synapse Software in 1984. Zaxxon is basically like a sci-fi version of Blue Max. It's an isometric shooter and a conversion from an old arcade game. Zaxxon has you making your way across the screen (in the classic up and down isometric fashion) and destroying as many ground targets as you can to rustle up points. Much like Blue Max, I suspect that nearly everyone who owned a C64 must have played Zaxxon at some point or other. It's a classic game of its type and still very playable.

BOULDER DASH (1984)

Label: First Star Software, Designer: Pepe Liepa, Chris Gray

In this 2D arcade game the player controls a man called Rockford digging through the ground looking for diamonds. He must ensure that through digging he does not loosen boulders - causing them to fall on him. There are other creatures to contend with too. If rocks fall on these creatures then they turn into diamonds which can be collected. When the diamonds have been collected an escape tunnel opens to the next level. There are 16 caves in all. After 4 caves there is a puzzle to be solved. The game had 5 difficultly levels.

Boulder Dash (a pun on the phrase "balderdash") is a classic game. The game was developed originally for Atari 8-bit computers and then ported to other home computers. There were numerous sequels, compilations and other versions and the game is still popular today on contemporary platforms. The C64 version looks very simplistic with basic graphics but it is a very addictive puzzle game. Tunnelling through the dirt and collecting the diamonds is very satisfying. The music and sound effects are great too. There were two sequels to Boulder Dash in 1985 and 1986 and both of these games are well worth playing if you love the original. It's basically just more Boulder Dash and what's wrong with that? The world always needs more Boulder Dash.

Boulder Dash is a great example of a game that doesn't look

awe-inspiring at first glance but has a great idea and concept behind it - thus making the gameplay fiendishly addictive. The Boulder Dash games are still huge fun today and thankfully the C64 versions were excellent. This is one of those games where you constantly find yourself being drawn back for just one more go. Boulder Dash remains amazingly playable and a true classic of home gaming.

BOUNDER (1986)

Label: Gremlin Graphics, Designer: Robert Toone

Bounder is a, on the face of it, preposterously silly and simple game in which you have to control a bouncing tennis ball up the screen as it makes its way up a course of paving stones. Naturally, these squares are not always fixed or safe so you may find your ball plunging to its death (the course, for some reason, seems to be up in the air). There are mystery squares too where you never quite know what you are going to get and also power squares which give you extra jumping abilities. There are of course many obstacles thrown your way also.

Bounder is colourful and attractive and though not the most ambitious game graphically it still looks nice. The game is maddeningly addictive - even when one becomes frustrated by that pesky tennis ball not always landing where you want it to go. A lot of C64 users thought this game was too tough and it is fair to say that the difficulty level amps up once you get past the early screens. If nothing else though this makes the game a challenge and gives it more playability. Bounder is an example of how you don't need the most elaborate or complex idea in the world to make a memorable game. This game earned a coveted Gold Medal award in ZZAP!64 and was highly praised on the C64.

It probably won't be everyone's cup of tea but Bounder is a challenging game that will constantly lure you back for one more go. The music, though quite good, is definitely an ear worm though and will rattle around in your head for days. The 1987 sequel Re-Bounder offers more of the same and is worth playing too (though unavoidably lacking the freshness of the original). There are enough new features in Re-Bounder to make it feel like a game in its own right so it is worth a look even if you played all through the first one and feel like you've had your fair share of Bounder escapades.

Bounder won't be for everyone but it is very addictive and if you like platform style games but sometimes feel as if they tend to merge into one another and become a trifle samey then Bounder at least offers a slight twist on this staple genre of retro gaming. Bounder was a clever idea for a game and thankfully the execution was competent enough to make the resulting game very playable and entertaining.

BRUCE LEE (1984)

Label: Datasoft, Designer: Ron J. Fortier

Bruce Lee is a platform game. The player is martial arts star Bruce Lee - who is exploring a wizard's chamber and attempting to find infinite wealth and the secret of immortality. There are twenty chambers in the game. Lanterns must be collected from each chamber to progress. Bruce is faced by two enemies - Yamo a green sumo wrestler and a Ninja. Also facing Bruce are various traps. When the game is completed it restarts with Yamo and the Ninja re spawning when they are killed and harder obstacles in the chambers.

Bruce Lee is a fun platform game with great gameplay. The graphics may seem a bit primitive but they are slightly strange - which suits the game. The underground levels are particularly mysterious. The Bruce Lee, Yamo and Ninja characters are very distinctive with some nice touches - it's quite funny to kick them around. It is a well designed platform game with great puzzles. One nice feature is that another player can control the enemy Yamo, or two players can collaborate and play Bruce. The game is not too difficult which makes it more playable and makes it a game that you will want to come back to. The game was originally written for the Atari 8 bit computers.

Bruce Lee is interesting because it combines a fighting game with a platform game - something which was quite new at the time. You don't get an elaborate number of fighting movies in the end but the combat serves its purpose and makes the game more enjoyable. Though fairly primitive in terms of graphics Bruce Lee has an amazingly addictive quality that makes you keep returning. To this day there are people who still go back and play this game each year despite the fact they've beaten it millions of times. You do wish the game was - ultimately - more difficult to beat but it's brilliant for what it is and one of the most memorable platform games of the C64 era.

Datasoft later tried to repeat their Bruce Lee formula with a Zorro game which was quite similar. Though it was fun, Zorro didn't quite manage to recapture the magic of Bruce Lee for some reason. Maybe it was the annoying looped music of Zorro that gave it a less glowing reception. An assault on the ears that is impossible to forget once experienced! Bruce Lee actually later got a re-release as a budget title on the C64. That was great value indeed.

BUBBLE BOBBLE (1987)

Label: Firebird, Designer: Fukio Mitsuji (original game), Stephen Ruddy (conversion coder)

Bubble Bobble is a C64 conversion of a Japanese arcade game from 1986. This conversion was much anticipated at the time and it didn't disappoint. In the game's story, "Baron Von Blubba" has kidnapped the brothers Bubby and Bobby's girlfriends and turned the brothers into Bubble Dragons, Bub and Bob. Bub and Bob have to complete one hundred levels in the Cave of Monsters in order to rescue them. This is a platform game with bags of colour and charm and fiendishly addictive stuff once you start playing it.

You can enclose the monsters in a bubble and if you successfully do this you pick up extra points. Though the C64 hardly needed another platform game an exception was definitely made in this case because Bubble Bobble was immediately engaging and charming and the sort of thing that even those who don't care for platform games could easily get addicted to. This game earned a coveted Gold Medal award from ZZAP!64 and is very highly regarded. What makes this game great too is the depth of the world it throws the player into.

One criticism of a lot of early C64 games is that they don't have many screens and can be beaten quite easily. That's certainly not the case with Bubble Bobble - which has one hundred screens and becomes progressively tough. It will certainly challenge even the most hardened platformer in the end and you'll find yourself eager to work out how to get all the bonuses and hidden screens.

Arcade conversions on the C64 could sometimes be hit or miss. Things like Space Harrier didn't translate especially well but Bubble Bobble is one of the best arcade transfers on the C64 and should have pleased anyone who was already a fan of this game.

The highest praise you can give Bubble Bobble is that it would probably even have some appeal to people who don't like platform games. This is a unique and enjoyable experience and one of the best platformers ever released on the C64. Bubble Bobble is terrific stuff on the whole and a superb game.

BUGGY BOY (1987)

Label: Elite, Designer: Dave Thomas

Buggy Boy is an off road racing game based on a 1985 Japanese arcade machine. The player drives a buggy around a track avoiding obstacles such as brick walls, fences and rocks. There are five tracks - Offroad, which needs to be completed five times, North , a wintry track with five subtracks; East has five subtracks; West and five subtracks and South has a desert landscape with five subtracks. There is a time limit to complete the tracks. The buggy also has to drive through gates. Flags and other bonuses can be collected. Driving through a time flag gives extra time for the stage to be completed.

This is a great conversion of the arcade game and a good C64 racer. It is very addictive. The difficulty level is about right with the later subtracks being more difficult. The animation is smooth and the graphics are fine. The controls are very responsive. There are also a variety of tracks in the game. All in all this is a fun C64 driving game. The game is known as Speed Buggy in North America. Buggy Boy earned a coveted Gold Medal award in ZZAP!64 (the most popular C64 magazine of the era) and proved to be a hig hit with gamers who enjoy racing games.

In terms of graphics, Buggy Boy is not the most amazing looking game on the C64 but the gameplay is excellent and this proves to be a fun experience on the whole. The buggy performs an impressive flip when it crashes and there are some nice touches like everything going dark when you enter a tunnel. The course designs in the game are very good and the game moves at a fast pace once you get going. The scrolling is fairly impressive too for the time. One of the interesting things about Buggy Boy is that it doesn't attempt to be a straight conversion of its arcade counterpart but rather seeks to be an interpretation. This was a logical move because while the C64 can't match the graphics of an arcade machine it could - in this case - replicate the fun and gameplay.

If you enjoyed Buggy Boy another game I'd recommend is The Great American Cross-Country Road Race. This is a 1985 game by Activision. The Great American Cross-Country Road Race is a racing game. The player is driving a car across America. Obstacles are road conditions, highway patrol, weather and lack of fuel. There are four different routes with different fastest time scoreboards. Los Angeles to New York, Seattle to Miami, and San Francisco to Washington, and a cross US route - visiting every city on the map.

Although the graphics and sound may be lacking The Great American Cross-Country Road Race is a wonderful C64 racing game. There are other driving games for the C64 that look very similar but this game has some aspects to make it different. There are a variety of weather conditions and even night-time driving. This means you really feel like you are on a journey. There are some nice touches too like the weather affecting the handling of the car. Also the gears need to be changed on the car. One other aspect is having to slow down for the police - who can be spotted via a radar. The game was originally written for Atari 8-bit systems. It was inspired by the 1976 film The Gumball Rally.

CALIFORNIA GAMES (1987)

Label: Epyx, Designer: Numerous

California Games is a multi-event sports game. The player chooses a sponsor rather than a country to compete for. The sponsors are real companies such as Casio and Kawasaki. The events are Half Pipe (skateboarding); Foot bag; surfing; skating; BMX and flying disc. Up to eight players can compete. This is another entry - the fifth - in Epyx's famous C64 sports series. You might have thought that after five entries this series might be getting a bit tiresome and samey but California

Games not only manages to freshen up the formula but at the time was the most graphically impressive of the sports games Epyx had produced. In short, California Games mre than justifies its own existence and is different enough from what came before not to feel like the same thing all over again.

California Games has a fun range of events. All are nicely animated and are fun to play. The surfing event seems to be the most popular in this game. One of the strengths of the Epyx series is that many of the events featured in the games could easily have been a game in their own right. This makes all the Epyx multi-event games feel more like great value for money and also gives you plenty of events to sink your teeth into in each individual game. The animations, backdrops, and scrolling in the various events in excellent. Epyx could have easily just plucked out something like the BMX event or surfing here and it would have made a perfectly decent game in its own right.

The graphics – especially the backdrops - are large and bold which shows the improvements on the early Epyx sports series. There is a good variety in the events too - the slightly unusual nature of the events is appealing and there's a nice sun drenched beach atmosphere. The usual Epyx excellent presentation is apparent here with lots of nice music and touches throughout the game. Although, on the face of it, the sports on offer sound less appealing than the other Epyx games (where you competed in athletics and winter events) the individual events are all fun to play and this is a highly polished and attractive game.

The series of sports simulations by Epyx for the C64 are justifiably famous and legendary and California Games is a more than worthy addition to the Epyx library. If you enjoyed the other Eypyx multi-sport games you should definitely enjoy this too. California Games is great fun on the whole and offers an interesting and entertaining change from the usual athletics events you tend to get in these multi-sports games. This game was a huge hit in 1987 and outsold the previous Epyx sports games. After less than two years of release California Games sold half a million copies.

THE CASTLES OF DOCTOR CREEP (1984)

Label: Broderbund, Designer: Ed Hobbs

The Castles of Doctor Creep is a platform arcade adventure game. The player has to escape each of thirteen medieval castles owned by Doctor Creep. The player chooses one of the castles then moves through the rooms or the castle to the exit. The player climbs ropes and ladders to solves puzzles in order to exit the room. Keys and doorbells are used. Teleport devices are sometimes used to navigate rooms. Conveyor belts, laser guns and forces fields are there to stop the player. In some rooms Frankenstein's monster and mummies must be trapped and killed. From the fourth castle on the puzzles become harder. There is a two player option with the two players working together.

This is a fun early platform game which has become a cult classic. Although the graphics are rudimentary they do have a great charm with the text and the different monsters being very colourful. The soundtrack with classical music adds to the game. It is a wonderful platform and puzzle game and the puzzles are fun to solve. There are lots of castles and rooms to play in.

There is a great horror atmosphere to go with the fun story to the game and castle names such as Carpathia, Lovecraft and Sylvania. The two player mode is a good addition to the game. Though it got mixed reviews upon release many gamers think this was one of the great unappreciated gems of the C64 era.

You might feel as if the C64 and other home gaming systems of the era had a few too many platform games in the end but if you do enjoy the genre then The Castles of Doctor Creep is one of the most playable and entertaining examples. This game doesn't have any incredibly original concepts or tremendously elaborate graphics but it does have an awful lot of old school charm and playability. The Castles of Doctor Creep is also one of the most enjoyable two player games on the C64 and scores highly for this alone. There are two hundred rooms in the game so it should keep you going for some time.

CHAMPIONSHIP WRESTLING (1986)

Label: Epyx, Designer: Richard Ditton, Elaine Ditton

Championship Wrestling is a professional wrestling game from Epyx. As this company were famed for their sports simulations, Championship Wrestling was much anticipated and - thankfully - turned out to be pretty good. C64 owners had largely been underwhelmed the previous year when Melbourne House released the wrestling game Rock'n Wrestle but Championship Wrestling was fortunately much better than that game. In Championship Wrestling the player chooses a wrestler and then has to beat the other eight wrestlers.

The wrestlers are K.C. Colossus, Purple Hays, Colonel Rooski, Prince Vicious, Zantoklaw, Zeke Weasel, The Berserker and howling Manslayer.

Each player has an energy bar. Making moves or taking hits depletes the energy bar. There are 25 moves. Up to eight players can compete

Wrestling was extremely popular in the 1980s and this is probably the best of the C64 wrestling games. The wrestlers seem to be based on real wrestlers - K.C. Colossus, for example, is patently similar to Hulk Hogan. The wrestlers are well depicted and there is a good range of them. Each wrestler is a well defined character - which is obviously important in wrestling as it is based on personalities as much as anything. A nice touch is that each wrestler has their own music theme. Maybe the chance to create a wrestler would have been a good option though.

The controls in Championship Wrestling are relatively easy to use with a big range of moves and special custom moves for each wrestler. The animations in the wrestling matches are fine - making the game fun to play.

Epyx tried and failed to get a World Wrestling Federation licence for the game but it doesn't really matter. Championship Wrestling is colourful, well designed, and is pretty good fun. I've never been hugely into wrestling games myself but this is one I definitely had fun with.

You can pin, slam, and drop kick your opponents and the background detail (complete with enthusiastic crowd) is very good. The presentation of the game is up to the high standards one would expect of Epyx and the actual combat is good fun. This is more or less all you'd want from a wrestling game in 1986 and the fact that the game has plenty of character and personality adds to the experience. You could have done with a few more moves to deploy in Championship Wrestling and the game isn't the longest but this was by far the best wrestling game on the C64.

Strangely, despite the appeal of wrestling on both sides of the Atlantic there were not that many wrestling games on the C64 (you'd have thought that Big Daddy's Wrestling would have been an obvious licenced game in Britain?) and most of them were absolutely terrible.

Championship Wrestling did at least give wrestling mad kids in the eighties one decent wrestling game to play. Championship Wrestling is an attractive and enjoyable game.

CREATURES 2 (1992)

Label: Thalamus, Designer: John Rowlands

Creatures 2: Torture Trouble is a puzzle and platform game. There are three islands in the game which contain a number of stages that have to completed. Bonus coins are gained during torture screens, interludes and island hopping levels which can be used for extra lives.

In Torture screens a number of tasks such as shooting switches or moving a rock must be made to complete a task in order to free children. In the Interludes a child is thrown by a monster and the player has to bounce the child to safety using a trampoline. In Demon screens three demons must be killed by kicking small animals into tubes. In Island hopping sequences the player has to swim across island transporting children to safety contending with monsters. The End sequence has a battle with a monster.

This is a sequel to Creatures - which was released in 1990. Creatures 2 is not a scrolling platform game like the original. It has one screen where all the action takes place. The gameplay is very addictive, although some have suggested that the underwater sections are mildly tiresome. The puzzles are fun to solve. The graphics are wonderful and very charming. The snow scenes in particular are very effective. The various characters look wonderful and - given the surreal aura of the game - there is great humour. It has amusingly bloody torture scenes with hilarious grisly deaths if the character is not saved. It is worth playing just for the opening credit sequence. Of course there is a fantastic music score for the game too. This is a late C64 release. It was released exclusively on the C64 in 1992.

Creatures 2 is one of the most impressive looking C64 games. The backdrops are incredibly varied and change often and the amount of colour on the screen is amazing. The cartoonish graphics have a lot of charm and personality too. By the time this game was released the C64 scene had seen better days and was slowly becoming a relic of the past but here was a reminder of just what an incredible machine it could and an enjoyable last hurrah. Creatures 2: Torture Trouble is fast, fun, funny, addictive and a great little game. The fact that this is a beautiful looking game too with some inventive and sparkling flourishes and effects is merely the icing on the cake.

DAN DARE: PILOT OF THE FUTURE (1986)

Label: Virgin games, Designer: Andy Wilson

Dan Dare: Pilot of the Future is an arcade adventure based on the comic strip hero Dan Dare. Dan Dare became famous in the pages of Eagle comics and was sort of like a British version of Buck Rogers. The best description for Dan Dare is Biggles in Space. In the game, Dan Dare must foil an attempt by arch villain the Mekon to project an asteroid at the Earth. Dan Dare must go to the asteroid and - as ever - foil the Mekon's plans. This will prove to be a rather challenging task - but then you probably wouldn't want it any other way.

Dan Dare: Pilot of the Future never seems to be mentioned when people discuss the best C64 games but one could argue that this is an unappreciated gem with some interesting gameplay mechanics. First of all the game looks amazing and is designed to look like a comic strip that has come to life. The colour is bold and vibrant and Dan himself has an enjoyable cartoon comic book quality. It's fun to explore the asteroid and the backdrops are consistently interesting and appealing. There are some nice touches too like the way you have to use a torch in a dark room. What really makes this game interesting is the blend of different game genres - which could have resulted in a dog's breakfast of a game but actually works beautifully here.

There is a platform game element to Dan Dare but it is also an adventure game with various puzzles to solve. There is even a beat em up element to the game because you have to engage in fisticuffs whenever you encounter one of the dastardly Treens. I love the detail in this game - like the flashing lights on the machines in a control room and the water effects. Interestingly, distinct versions of this game were made for different systems. So this game is a special new C64 only version and not a direct replica of the Amstrad or Spectrum versions. I can't vouch for this game on other systems but the C64 version is great fun.

The end of the game has you finally confronting the Mekon and he's clearly not too happy to see Dan because he starts lobbing grenades at you. Dan Dare: Pilot of the Future is one of those games that is very likeable because you can see that a love of love and hard work has gone into it. It's one of the best examples of a licenced game on the C64. The mix of attractive comic book graphics and melange of gameplay styles make Dan Dare: Pilot of the Future a memorable experience. It probably won't be everyone's cup of tea but Dan Dare: Pilot of the Future is a very well made and interesting game. One minor quibble though is that the game has no music - which is a shame.

DEFENDER OF THE CROWN (1987)

Label: Cinemaware, Designer: Kellyn Beeck

Defender of the Crown is a strategy game set in England during the middle ages - in 1149. In the game different people are fighting for control of the crown. The player chooses a Saxon - from Wilfred of Ivanhoe, Cedric of Rotherwood, Geoffrey Longsword, or Wolfric the Wild. The enemies fighting the Saxons for control of England are the Normans. The player has to defeat the enemies armies and take their castles to gain their territory. Territory can be won in jousting conceptions.

This is a classic C64 game by Cinemaware - who made a series of classic adventure strategy games such as Rocket Ranger. It was first produced for the Amiga in 1986 and used as a showcase for the advanced graphics of the machine. The C64 naturally has inferior graphics to the Amiga version but the version of this game made for the C64 is is still outstanding and atmospheric. It has a series of fun mini-games such as jousting and firing rocks via catapult at the enemy castle. The strategy element of acquiring parts of the map and building up an army is addictive. A memorable part is a love scene after a damsel is rescued at an enemies castle.

Defender of the Crown is a wonderfully cinematic game and was one of the most ambitious games of its era. It still looks pretty good even to this day. The game is a nice mix of strategy and actual gameplay. Many people think that the C64 version, though not quite as pretty as the Amiga version, actually had better gameplay. This game is a great example of what the C64 was capable of. One might argue that the gameplay might not have the most depth and that Defender of the Crown is simply a showcase for fancy new graphics but this is preposterously unfair as there is still an excellent game at the heart of the impressive visual design.

Defender of the Crown is one of those games that anyone who owned an Amiga or C64 simply had to play and they were far from disappointed when they sampled it for themselves. You'll never forget the beautiful static images or that nifty 3D jousting.

Defender of the Crown is a true cinematic experience and one of the most ambitious games ever released on the C64. This is one of those late eighties games that you simply HAD to play.

THE DETECTIVE GAME (1986)

Label: Argus Press Software, Designer: Sam Manthorpe

The Detective Game, developed by Sam Manthorpe and
released in 1986 by Argus Press Software, stars Inspector
Snide, a hard boiled detective from Scotland Yard who is
called to investigate a case in a huge luxurious villa. The year is
1974 and the grouchy old millionaire Angus McFungus has
just died in mysterious circumstances. Snide, being a grown
up inspector who needs no backup, goes in alone to investigate
the villa in order to find out what happened. Unfortunately, as
these things usually go, it's not long before the other guests
begin to start dropping like flies and it's up to Snide to not
only survive but also solve this perplexing whodunit.

This is definitely a Cluedo inspired game - even the cast of
usual suspects seems to mirror those of the board game, along
with a pretty unsympathetic butler. Naturally, the first order of
business is to collect pieces of evidence. These are individually
stored in bags and there are ten of them to collect throughout
the story and only then can Snide finger the culprit. The
Detective Game is played in real time, or at least a reasonable
facsimile since certain events will not come to pass if the
player is not exploring and moving around the house.
Standing still will run out the clock but will not cause certain
events to happen. Overall, the player has two hours and twenty
minutes of real time to solve the mystery or else it's game over.

This is a fun game on the whole and something a bit different
from blasting aliens and sports simulations. This is a graphical
adventure more than anything and although it didn't set the
world alight in terms of its original reviews it later established
itself as a cult favourite thanks to its likeable and colourful
presentation and engaging mix of subtle and not so subtle
puzzles. This can be quite a tricky game to complete but I
daresay you can probably find a walkthrough somewhere now
if you get really stuck. If you like detective stories and

graphical adventures then you should enjoy this game a lot. It has plenty of atmosphere and a nice sense of humour.

DROPZONE (1984)

Label: US Gold, Designer: Archer MacLean

Dropzone is inspired by the arcade game Defender. On Jupiter's moon a scientific research base is under alien attack. The player controls a man in a jetpack armed with a laser, three smart bombs and cloaking device to rescue the scientists. Scientists are in survival pods on the surface. The pods must be picked up and deposited in a silo - the dropzone. This is classic shoot em up game. Although the graphics do look simple at first they suit the game and the animation scrolling is very good. The movement of the jetpack man is enjoyable - with the game taking into account the gravity - and easy to control even though the game is quite fast paced. There are lots of sound effects, explosions and effects which add to the atmosphere. The laser and other weapons are very satisfying to use.

Dropzone works really well because the movement and controls feel smooth - which is essential in a game as fast and furious as this. Although the game is quite difficult at first, over time the player will get into the obstreperous rhythm of Dropzone and begin to anticipate the enemy attacks. Once you begin to master this game somewhat it becomes a lot of fun. The ability of the player to race along whichever side of the screen they choose is of course a lot of fun and gives the enjoyable impression of freedom of movement.

An early Defender clone on the C64 was a game called Guardian. Dropzone essentially takes Guardian and amps everything up to eleven (as Nigel Tufnel might say) - creating a slick and satisfying shooter which head and shoulders above anything else at the time.

Dropzone oozes class and the impressive and fast paced graphics are merely the backdrop for what really matters - fantastic gameplay. Dropzone is one of those games that most C64 users will always remember. This was one of the gold standards of the machine and a timeless shooter that is as fast and frantic to play today as it was in 1984. Dropzone is unquestionably one of the classics of the C64 era and a great game. The only quibble one might have with Dropzone is that more variety in the backdrops would have been nice. The fact that this game can be very tough seems like an advantage now in that it makes Dropzone a challenge. This will prove a test for even the most hardened shoot em up fanatic.

If you love Dropzone you should also play the 1988 Thalamus game Retrograde. This game is very reminiscent of Dropzone at times in that you control a spaceman blasting everything in sight and scrolling in both directions but Retrograde then introduces more traditional shoot em up mechanics and even platform elements as the world the game takes place in opens up. The graphics are bright and attractive in Retrograde and it's a really fun shooter for those who have a sweet tooth for blasting action. Another game really worth playing if you like Defender/Dropzone style action is Jeff Minter's 1986 game Iridis Alpha. Iridis Alpha is fast, frantic, brilliant, and completely bonkers.

THE EIDOLON (1985)

Label: Lucasfilm, Designer: Charlie Kellner

The player in this game has a 19th century vehicle which has been found in a laboratory. On looking at the vehicle the player is transported to another dimension and trapped in a cave complex. Creatures in the cave are woken by the energy from the vehicle. The player must navigate thorough the cave levels defeating a dragon at the end of each level. There are eight levels and energy orbs have to be collected. They are in four different colours: yellow, green, red and blue.

The creatures try to absorb the energy of the Eidolon. Green orbs can turn enemies into other enemies. Blue orbs can freeze enemies. Each level has three diamonds guarded by an enemy. When the enemies are defeated and diamonds collected the player moves onto the next level. The game ends when dragons are defeated or the game time runs out.

This early Lucasfilm is a very atmospheric and creepy game. The vehicle seems reminiscent of the Victorian time travelling machine in H.G.Wells's book (and the 1960 film adaption) The Time Machine. The range of creatures are well presented: they are large and nicely animated. You never know which creature is going to be around the corner. It is presented almost in the style of a first person shooter with great 3D effects as you move through the caves. There are some nice sound effects too.

The Lucasfilm game Raid on Fractulus used fractal technology to depict mountains. For this game the mountains were simply inverted to create the caves. The Eidolon might seem fairly rudimentary to modern eyes and it isn't the fastest game in the world but this was pretty amazing stuff for 1985. If one falls for the atmosphere of the game it is a very immersive experience. The interesting thing about Lucasfilm is that their games seemed to push the limits of the C64 to the very edge. These very cinematic and ambitious games were probably TOO ambitious for the C64 at the time but this quality makes them fascinating at times.

The Eidolon is just a very interesting mystery adventure game with vintage sci-fi and horror trappings. From a modern perspective the speed of the game is rather sedate and those monsters are hardly detailed but this was all very impressive in 1985 and those monsters were pretty damn terrifying at the time. This game is a fascinating early example of someone trying to do a first person game and - given the era - it's a pretty good attempt too. The Eidolon probably won't be for everyone but if you like immersive games with a slower pace then this remains good stuff.

ELITE (1985)

Label: Firebird, Designer: David Braben, Ian Bell

Elite is a famous space/simulation game. The game is viewed from the spaceship cockpit. There are vector graphics to convey the action. The player is Commander Jameson (the name can be changed) who travels through space as an astronaut and trader. There are eight galaxies to explore and the player starts at a space station with 100 credits. The first ship is a Cobra Mark III. Credits are gained through activities such as piracy, military missions, trade, asteroid mining and bounty hunting. Ships can be upgraded with items such as better weapons and more cargo capacity. The game is open ended and creates a massive world for the player to explore.

Elite is often cited as the first space flight simulator. Those looking for an action game are liable to be disappointed by Elite but it is an immersive experience for those who enjoy strategy and a more realistic type of sci-fi game. There is shooting and space dog fights though. The vector graphics seem simplistic today but they were effective at the time and in many ways give Elite its unique look and atmosphere. Elite is a classic and important game. It's a cross between a trading strategy game and a 3D shoot em up. C64 owners will probably never forget the fiddly and occasionally frustrating task of docking at a space station.

The key to Elite is how much time you put in. If you put the effort in, learn to dock reliably, and begin trading then this game offers an impressive depth of gameplay and is astonishing for the world building it creates in terms of its fictional universe. If you just give Elite a quick look though you are liable to barely scratch the surface at all and not really understand the game. There were a number of sequels and updates to Elite over the years and these should be fun to explore for anyone who enjoyed the original game. If you like Elite you should probably check out a 1987 Firebird game called Tau Ceti. This game is sort of like a more modern version of Elite and although it doesn't have the same depth of gameplay and strategy it is an interesting and well made game.

If you liked elite you should also definitely play Mercenary: Escape from Targ - a 1985 game from Novagen. This game was originally designed for the Atari and feels like a blood relative to Elite with its vector style graphics. In the game you crash land on a planet called Targ and must find a way to escape. Matters are complicated though by the presence of two races - one benign and another more warlike invader (that's more or less the plot of the first classic Unreal game! in 1998!) Mercenary: Escape from Targ is a very rewarding game if you take the time to get into it and it is something of a computing marvel in that you can't believe a game this huge could fit inside the C64. The graphics are unavoidably dated today but this was an amazing looking game for the time.

If you like these types of games you should certainly investigate the 1991 Melbourne House game Supremacy: Your Will Be Done. Supremacy: Your Will Be Done is an icon driven strategy game. In the game the player - the ruler of the Epsilon system - has to create and protect colonies on planets. An enemy is trying to do the same and must be defeated. There are four skill levels and each skill level has a different enemy race: Hitotsu, Mittsu, Yottsu and Futatsu. The player first chooses which planetary system to enter. The planetary systems have progressively more planets, better spacecraft and more demanding computer AI as the game progresses. In a system the player and the computer opponent have one planet. The player has to colonize the planets before the opponent.

Planets have to be terraformed, supped with food and energy, and taxes raised. The military on the planets must be funded and equipped. The game is won by taking the enemies' starbase. Supremacy: Your Will Be Done is a great late C64 game with very good graphics and music. It is a strategy game in the vein of Civilisation. There is a lot of gameplay with four different opponents to beat and numerous planets to take over. There is also good variety with the game with different approaches able to be taken. The icon system and various screens are easy to use. The game was originally written for the 16 bit Atari ST and Amiga computers in 1990.

Another game you should try if you like Elite is the 1986 Accolade game Psi-5 Trading Company. Psi-5 Trading Company is a strategy and trading game. This game has some obvious similarities to Elite. The player is in charge of a cargo ship in space. The player is also in charge of a crew and has to transport cargo through outer space facing dangers from pirates. A crew is selected to man the ship. A different person is needed for weapons, navigation, scanning, repairs and Engineering. Crew choices include aliens and robots. Thirty crew members can be chosen from. Each possible crew member has different abilities and characteristics and are shown in a dossier which can be viewed. The crew chosen affect the success of the mission and are given orders to run the ship. The game is lost if the ship is looted or severely damaged. A game is won if some cargo is delivered. On screen there is a space view screen, a crew member screen, a message screen and various status buttons.

Psi-5 Trading Company is a fun space trading game where one can captain a ship like in one of those space science-fiction shows such as Red Dwarf or Star Trek. The graphics are colourful and there are a nice range of crew members to see on the screen. There is great humour too in their messages and depictions - especially when they start to get stressed and lose control. The game is a crisis management simulation with the player having to manage the ship as it is attacked, looted etc. Crew member choices and the players decisions affect the success of the mission which makes the game very satisfying to play. Psi-5 Trading Company is an interesting and well made game that had appeal for those who like some strategy and humour with their games. If nothing else Psi-5 Trading Company was a change from endless shooting games.

EMLYN HUGHES INTERNATIONAL SOCCER (1988)

Label: Audiogenic, Designer: Graham Blighe

Emlyn Hughes International Soccer is a football simulation. It is named after Emlyn Hughes - the former England and Liverpool footballer. He was a captain on the quiz show A Question of Sport too. The C64 was festooned with soccer games and many of them were dreadful but this game is definitely the gold standard when it comes to C64 football simulations. The game is a side on football game. Team names, players and kit colours can be edited. Players have player ratings and league and cup competitions are available as well as one off friendlies.

This is a fantastic football game and one of the best sports sims on the C64. The game is very playable and the ball can be moved around the pitch using the joystick - the ball can be kicked in 5 different directions by holding the fire button down and putting the joystick in the direction you want the ball to go and then releasing the fire button.

Other moves such as sliding tackles and diving headers also feature in the game.

This game feels like an improvement on another C64 classic called International Soccer. In International Soccer the ball could only be kicked along the ground. It was really satisfying when playing Emlyn Hughes for the first time to boot the ball down the pitch in the air! The graphics are not that ground breaking in Emlyn Hughes but the gameplay more than makes up for this. The players are nicely animated and you always feel like the ball is easy to control and pass - which are obviously necessary qualities in any soccer game.

The thing that really kills a lot of the weaker C64 football games is the fact that they are too slow. There is nothing more frustrating than a football game where the players move like snails and the ball has all the weight and control of a brick. Happily, the players and ball in Emlyn Hughes all flow smoothly and quickly so there is always a good sense of pace. Emlyn Hughes International Soccer has great gameplay and controls and remains a satisfying experience for anyone who enjoys football games. Emlyn Hughes International Soccer is great stuff and arguably the greatest football game for the C64.

ENTOMBED (1985)

Label: Ultimate, Designer: Dave Thomas

Entombed is an isometric action adventure game. The player is adventurer Sir Arthur Pendragon - who is attempting to escape an Egyptian tomb before the oxygen runs out. Arthur must solve various puzzles and fight off enemies using a whip. There are dark areas of the tomb which can be seen using a torch. The player has an energy bar which is depleted when touched by enemies. Killing a crow will replenish the bar. If the energy bar empties the game ends. The tomb has seven levels.

Entombed is a charming Indiana Jones style misadventure game. There are mysterious enemies to fight: mummies, scorpion/basilisk, fat flies and thin flies. The graphics were called a little blocky but they work here and add to the charm. The animations are very good though. Arthur is distinctive character and the game has plenty of charm and character. There are atmospheric ancient Egyptian themes backgrounds and some nice detail in the them. Another nice aspect is the different colours in the various rooms. There are great sound effects with - for example - the footsteps, although a lack of music. There are interesting if mildly difficult puzzles to solve.

The game is a sequel to The Staff of Karnath (1985). Another sequel featuring Sir Arthur Pendragon and similar gameplay and graphics was Blackwyche - which was set on a haunted galleon. Entombed is a very addictive game and you'll be eager to explore all the different rooms and levels. The colourful and attractive visual presentation of the game is very pleasing and mitigates the blocky character designs and animations. This is the sort of game you can easily play for hours when you first load it up as the exploration aspect to the game is a lot of fun.

Entombed received a very good reception when it appeared on the C64 and earned a deserved 93% in ZZAP!64

FORBIDDEN FOREST & BEYOND THE FORBIDDEN FOREST (1983)

Label: Cosmi, Desinger: Paul Norman

Forbidden Forest is an adventure/action game. The player is an archer who is in a forest full of monsters such as giant spiders, frogs, dragons, snakes and wizards. The final enemy is a Demogorgon.

There are four difficulty levels: Innocent, Trooper, Daredevil and Crazy. The player has three lives and 40 arrows: they are refreshed at the end of each level. Level 1 involves huge black spiders. Level 2 has giant wasps. Level 3 has monster frogs. Level 4 has a dragon. Level 5 Ghosts and skeletons. Level 6 has a giant snake. Level 7 is the Demogorgon.

If the player wins then the game starts with the next highest difficulty.

This is a very creepy and atmospheric game with scary

monsters and a great horror style music score. It is one of the earliest computer games to feature animated blood. The graphics are rudimentary and blocky but they add to the charm. They are almost in the style of an abstract art painting - adding to the surreal atmosphere of the game. Also, the game has parallax scrolling, a day night cycle and some of the monsters move forward from the background. This is, despite its fairly ordinary looking graphics, a very groundbreaking cinematic game for 1983. The programmer Paul Norman wanted to create a cinematic style experience and his monsters were inspired by the films Night of the Demon (1957), Jason and the Argonauts (1983) and Mysterious Island (1961).

Norman had nearly finished the game when the company he was working for Synchro went out of business. Luckily another company - Cosmi - hired him after they saw Forbidden Forest and he was able to complete the game.

A sequel called Beyond the Forbidden Forest was released in 1985. This game is arguably even better than the original and has a remarkably creepy soundtrack and atmosphere. These two games are great early examples of horror survival - though with an arcade rather than strategy or adventure bent. The sequel slightly changes the perspective of the character you play and is generally felt to have been an improvement in terms of gameplay. Though the graphics look basic today you'll still jump out of your seat when the monsters and giant spiders enter the fray.

The two Forbidden Forest games are among the very best examples of horror games on the C64 because they are both atmospheric and scary. The gameplay is decent enough too to keep you engaged and immersed in the experience. Theses two games definitely show their age today in terms of graphics but they were striking pieces of design for the era and both deserve a mention in any discussion of the most memorable and arresting games produced for the C64.

FORT APOCALYPSE (1982)

Label: Synapse Software, Designer: Steve Hales

Fort Apocalypse is an Atari game that was ported to the C64. It was inspired by games like Choplifter. Fort Apocalypse has the player controlling a helicopter that is attempting to rescue hostages in a huge barracks that appears to be underground. You have to pick up the hostages and shoot various enemies. The chopper has freedom of movement and can go in any direction. Though the gameplay sounds simple you have to be very careful in how you pick up the hostages and can only carry so many. There are also numerous obstacles in your path including lasers, crushers, and walls (which can be shot away). You will have to maintain control of the chopper at all times if you are to navigate the screens and complete the missions.

Do you remember how in the introduction to this book I complained about the game Airwolf and said it was one of my most disappointing experiences on the C64? Well, Fort Apocalypse is basically the game that Airwolf copied and tried to be. Both of these games essentially have you controlling a helicopter and trying to make your way through what appears to be a giant cave system as you rescue hostages. Here is the salient difference though - Fort Apocalypse is fun to play while Airwolf is not.

You always feel in control of the helicopter in Fort Apocalypse and the gameplay is challenging without feeling too frustrating. You have more room to manouvre too. Airwolf is the complete opposite. You never feel in control of that damn helicopter in Airwolf and the obstacles and hazards are too intricate and unfair. Airwolf is simply too claustrophobic in terms of its surroundings. Fort Apocalypse is a classic game while Airwolf is simply annoying. Though it might not be much to look at graphically, Fort Apocalypse is a fun and addictive game that scores highly on gameplay. It's a fairly simple idea for a game but very enjoyable to play. Fort

Apocalypse is an oldie but a goodie and one of the most purely playable and entertaining games from the very early years of the C64.

FRANKIE GOES TO HOLLYWOOD (1985)

Label: Ocean, Designer: Dave Colclough, Graham Everitt

This is a strange but excellent game which uses the Liverpudlian pop band Frankie goes to Hollywood as a licence. The game is an arcade adventure in which you have to decipher the identity of a killer and complete a series of tasks (essentially mini-games) in which the goal is to prove worthy of entering the Pleasuredome. What does all this have to do with the pop group you might be asking yourself. Well, not a lot really but it doesn't matter. This is one of the most innovative games of the C64 era and frequently crops up near the top of lists which cite the greatest C64 games ever made.

This is a rather abstract game quite unlike anything else you could play at the time. If you like arcade adventures full of puzzles then this should be right up your alley. Frankie goes to Hollywood is one of those games that you can't make head nor tail of when you first play it but it begins to make more sense when you put some hours into it. It's a very entrancing sort of game with great music as you wander through a number of houses and complete various arcane tasks. This is a very distinctive looking game with the different sections supplying a welcome dose of variety. The game is very surreal and deliberately strange and this is all part of the charm.

Legend had it at the time that it was impossible to defeat the game but this is not true and it can be completed. Frankie goes to Hollywood is a game that is better played than described and a fairly unique experience. This was one of the most surprising and inventive C64 games of its era. It probably won't be everyone's cup of tea but it's a fascinating experience if nothing else. Frankie goes to Hollywood is remarkable because it's something of a confusing mess at first glance but then falls into place and begins to make sense. There is some genius design in this game and once you begin to get the hang of things it becomes very addictive.

Even back in the 1980s it was very difficult in games to come up with something original because most ideas had already been done - and more than once too. Frankie goes to Hollywood was a nice reminder though that it was still possible to come up something quite unlike anything you'd ever seen before and give gamers an unusual and unexpected gaming experience that felt fresh and fascinating. Frankie goes to Hollywood is easily a game which could have turned out to be a disaster or licence cash grab but this wasn't the cae at all. The resulting game was truly one of the best C64 games of its era.

GAUNTLET (1986)

Label: US Gold, Designer: Bob Armour, Bill Allen, Alex Thirlwall

Gauntlet is a top down 2D shoot em up fantasy dungeon crawl shoot em up game.

The player chooses one of four characters who are trapped in a maze of dungeons trying to escape. Warrior: strong and resilient; slow and not very gifted with magic. Valkyrie: a cross-section of everything; in no category particularly strong. Eleven: fast but weak. Mage: strong in magic, fast, but quite weak.

There are 512 dungeons and the player must locate the exit on each level. The player must survive, collecting treasures and other items to score points.

The Monsters include guests, grunts, demons, stone throwers, sorcerers, and Death. Weapons to kill the monsters include the axe, sword, fireballs and arrows. Magic can be used. The player has 2000 health points. Touching a monster will deplete health. Amulets can be collected that make the player invisible, allow teleportation, and give the player more powers. Food gives more energy. A two player option is available.

Gauntlet is a conversion of the classic and popular arcade game released in 1985. This is a good conversion of the arcade game although it lacks the four player element and some of the excitement of playing in the arcade and having to put money in the machine to restore health. The graphics and animations are fine for the game. There are clearly defined different characters in the game. It's a very simple game and very addictive with lots of action.

The port of Gauntlet was much anticipated in 1986 because the arcade version was so popular. Happily, this home port didn't disappoint. Gauntlet was a big influence on Doom in the way that one must fight monsters to get out of rooms and unlock doors. In many ways Doom is like a 3D version of Gauntlet - albeit with more sci-fi and violence.

Gauntlet is classic and timeless fun and though the presentation might be fairly simple but it is very effective. This game probably comes to life the most when more than one player is involved but it's still a decent experience if one is playing alone and was rightly regarded to be one of the best arcade conversions on the C64 at the time. Gauntlet is very addictive and more or less all you could hope in terms of a conversion. You might find the gameplay a trifle samey in the end but by that stage you should have got full full value out of the game anyway. If you like Dungeons & Dragons and all things eighties arcade you should enjoy this game.

There were two sequels to Gauntlet and both of them are well worth playing if you like the original.

GHOSTBUSTERS (1984)

Label: Activision, Designer: David Crane

Ghostbusters is an adaption of the 1984 film of the same name. In the game the player must set up a company to catch ghosts. The player is given money for a vehicle. A grid of the city shows all the ghost activity. When the player moves to a place in the grid an over head street view is shown of the player driving to the site. A spectral vacuum can be used to suck up any ghosts. At the location two men must manoeuvre a ghost into a trap using beams. Successfully catching a ghost earns money. If the ghost is not caught one of three members of the team may be incapacitated. The player must return to the base occasionally to empty ghost traps and treat injured members of the team.

To win the game the player must guide two men past the Stay Puft Marshmallow Man (a giant marshmallow man) into the Temple of Zuul, or earn more money than the total spent on equipment before the PK energy level (create by ghosts) reaches 9999. After completing the game, an account number is given allowing the player to carry over money into the next game. Though this all sounds rather complex the gameplay is not that difficult once you get into the swing of things.

This is a fun licenced game conversion of the film. It has colourful graphics and there are many fun elements to the gameplay. Making money to buy different cars and equipment is good. Controlling the Ghostbuster team catching a ghost with an energy beam is fun too. By today's standards it is a simple game but by 1984 C64 standards it is a fun strategy/adventure game which captures the atmosphere of the original Ghostbuster film. One might say the inclusion of Ghostbusters on this list is slightly contentious because some would argue it isn't a great game but the attempt to capture the spirit of the film is admirable and this game is good undemanding fun.

Licenced games could often be dire and shoddy but you can
see that a lot of effort has gone into this Ghostbusters game. It
isn't perfect but for pure nostalgia alone is worthy of a place in
the hallowed halls of the C64's most famous games. I can
remember having a lot of fun playing this and catching the
ghosts and the music is good too. This game probably doesn't
have the replayability of the truly classic C64 games but if you
are a fan of Ghostbusters you should have a pretty good time
with this.

GHOSTS 'N GOBLINS (1986)

Label: Elite, Designer: Chris Butler

Ghosts 'n Goblins is a jump and run scrolling platform game.
In the game the player is a knight named Arthur. He must
battle through the undead to rescue kidnapped Princess Prin-
Prin from the Demon King Astaroth. Arthur's armour
determines his health and magic. Better armour and weapons
can be found in treasure chests. There are four levels divided
into two parts - Cemetery and forest (woods), Ice palace and
ghost town, Clouds (or sky) and fire bridge, Underground
labyrinth and demon castle. To move to the second part of a
level a death bird must be defeated. At the end of a level a
stronger demon such as a dragon needs to be defeated. At the
end of the game the princess must be rescued from a large
dragon. After completion of the game it starts again but with a
higher difficulty level.

This is based on a Japanese arcade game released by Capcom
in 1985. it's a classic game that has spawned lots of remakes
and sequels. The game has a great setting with lots of great
monsters to fight - such as zombies, ghosts, demons and even
shooting carnivores. It is a great conversion from the arcade
game although a few of the levels were missing. Ghosts 'n
Goblins has great graphics and animated monsters. There are
some nice touches - one fun part is that if Arthur loses his

armour he is left wearing his underpants. Be warned this is a very difficult game but it does have bags of atmosphere and will keep you going for a while.

Ghosts 'n Goblins is probably one of the best platform shooters on the C64 and still looks pretty good as far as theses types of games go (although there are a few glitches here and there). Arcade conversions on the C64 were constricted by what was possible. For example, to make an accurate conversion of something like Space Harrier was all but impossible on the C64. Ghosts 'n Goblins, as a fairly humble side scroller, was a different kettle of fish though and even if you had been pumping coins into this at the seaside arcade you would have been pretty happy with this C64 version and delighted at the chance to get that Ghosts 'n Goblins experience in the comfort of your own home.

GO FOR THE GOLD! (1986)

Label: Americana, Designer: Michael F.C. Crick

Go for the Gold! is a multi-event sports game. The events are diving, 110m sprint, 110m hurdles, archery, long jump and weightlifting (2-hand snatch. clean and jerk). Up to six players can compete. This is also known as HES Games (released originally in 1984) and World Games.

This is a wonderful, colourful multi-event sports game. There were many (too many you might venture) games of this type on the C64 but Go for The Gold! is good enough to justify its own existence and stand as a terrific game in its own right without drawing comparisons to other staples like Summer Games and Hyper Sports.

There are a range of fun events in this game. The graphics are quite blocky but colourful and the animations are good. The on screen competitors are quite large which makes a change from many other sports sims. There is a slightly different approach taken too in the perspective of some of the events. One nice touch is that the player can choose the colour of their outfit. There is an action replay too. There is some joystick waggling involved in the sprinting events though - which is always sort of annoying.

Go for the Gold! is a lot of fun on the whole and another of those multi-sport sims which the C64 felt positively festooned with at times. Thankfully though this is one of the better ones. Although this is not quite as polished as the Epyx sports sims, the large character animations and good gameplay make it an excellent game. The crowd animations are also quite good in this game. I like the way everyone applauds when you successfully lift a weight!

It's a slight shame though that you don't get a few more events in this. A javelin or pole vault would have been a nice addition. These quibbles aside though this is a fun game for those who have a sweet tooth for the multi-event sports games. Even if you have played Summer Games II and Hyper Sports this is still well worth playing.

A game worth a mention here is the 1984 Activision game Decathlon. In this game you compete in various (and familiar) events like the hurdles and pole vault. Activision's Decathlon game has some pretty good gameplay, decent graphics, and is generally worth a look if you like multi-sports games. The only annoying thing about the game was that it required some dreaded joystick waggling.

As for Daley Thompson's Decathlon (released by Ocean in 1985), though I had fun with the game at the time it dated very fast and was quickly supplanted by a number of more polished and ambitious C64 sports games (of which Epyx were naturally at the top table). Daley Thompson's Decathlon is really only one for C64 completists these days. You'd be better off playing any number of C64 multi-event sports games instead.

GRAHAM GOOCH'S TEST CRICKET (1985)

Label: Audiogenic, Designer: Andrew Calver

Graham Gooch's Test Cricket is a cricket simulation. Limited overs or two innings games of cricket can be played. The player can choose from squads of players or create and save custom teams. The gameplay has arcade mode where the player must choose which shot to play and press fire at the correct time. The joystick is waggled for bowling speed. There are 9 skill levels. In the simulation mode the player makes tactical decision - e.g. to be attacking or defensive.

Graham Gooch's Test Cricket is a fun and strangely relaxing simulation of cricket and the arcade mode is entertaining to use. The simulation gives less control over the players as the player just chooses to be aggressive or defensive but this allows for the game to be almost a text cricket simulation - which sounds boring but was very appealing to big cricket fans. The graphics are a bit basic even for 1985, but they are fine for the game.

There are details on the internet of an updated version of this game with new graphics and fielding system that was due to be released in 1991. This new version was sadly not released in the end but a new version of this game was released near the end of the C64's days in about 1993. This version had coloured clothing and a white ball which makes the game more fun.

Graham Gooch's Test Cricket was fun for cricket fans and a personal favourite of mine. I even liked playing out a one day game in what felt like real time! If you like cricket then you could get hours of fun out of this game. If you hate cricket then you should probably approach this game with a bit more caution though. I don't know if it had something to do with the perceived popularity of the sport (though cricket was much more popular and mainstream in the eighties than it is today because it used to be live on free television all the time - the idiots who run cricket in England now have long since sold their souls to SKY and turned it into a minority sport) or was simply because cricket is tricky to adapt but cricket games were thin on the ground in the C64 era.

There were plenty of baseball games (obviously from the American companies) on the C64 but cricket games were a rarer beast. For this reason I've always had a big soft spot for Graham Gooch's Test Cricket because not only is it a cricket game it is also a pretty good game in and of itself to boot.

Graham Gooch's Test Cricket won't be for everyone but if you are looking for a decent cricket game on the C64 then this is the obvious one to play.

GRAND PRIX CIRCUIT (1989)

Label: Accolade, Designer: Numerous

Grand Prix Circuit is a Formula One motor racing simulation. The player chooses between a Williams, McLaren or Ferrari car. Each car has its own characteristics as regards to chassis model, engine revolution speed, gear shift, tyre producer and weight. The player can race for fun, have a single race, or a season of races. For real races there is a qualification round which determines the place on the starting grid.

There are eight tracks with their own characteristics : Brazil - Autodromo Int. Nelson Piquet (Rio de Janeiro), Monaco - Circuit de Monaco, Canada - Circuit Gilles Villeneuve (Montreal), USA - Detroit Grand Prix Circuit, England - Silverstone Circuit, Germany – Hockenheimring, Italy - Autodromo Nazionale Monza, Japan - Suzuka International Racing Course.

This is a very good Formula One sim and a progression from

early games such as Pitstop II. The salient progression here is that this game places one inside the cockpit so you get a true first-person perspective. The graphics and scrolling are very good for the C64. It is very playable with multiple options. There are different cars to choose from. There is a single race or season option - as well as an option to race for fun. There is actual racing in the game with other drivers.

One nice touch is that there are nine imaginary drivers to take part in the season and race against with names such as Nigel Levins and Gregory Kwok. This creates a fantasy Formula One world for the game and helps with the longevity and playability of the game. There are different difficulty levels - on the highest levels there are gear changes which must be executed correctly to make the car is not damaged. There is a highscore table too.

The game is nicely presented with great graphics in the menu screens and a memorable theme. There were many racing games for the C64 and it this is probably technically the best one, although some of the others maybe more fun.

Although the scrolling these days won't seem especially smooth or rapid, Grand Prix Circuit looked amazing at the time and the chance to experience a driving game from a first person vantage point was quite novel.

If you like this game you should also check out the 1986 Geoff Crammond C64 game Revs. Revs, like Grand Prix Circuit, is more of a realistic take on the racing game and gives you a first person perspective as the driver. Revs is not quite as polished looking as Grand Prix Circuit but one might argue that the game is better at conveying speed.

Revs is very engrossing when you are in the thick of a race and jostling with other drivers for position.

THE GREAT GIANA SISTERS (1987)

Label: Rainbow Arts, Designer: Armin Gessert

The Great Giana Sisters is a jump and run game. In the game Giana from Milano has a nightmare and finds herself in a strange world filled with creatures who want to prevent her from returning home. To return home she must find a jewel. On the quest for the jewel she collects diamonds and other extras. There are 33 levels. Each level must be completed in 100 seconds. At the end of each levels bosses must be defeated. The game can be two player with the second player as Giana's sister Maria.

This is a classic game in the platform genre for the C64. It looks very pleasant and colourful with great sprites. The game takes place in a wonderful dream like world and the controls are easy to use. It is a highly addictive and playable game and is similar to the NES classic Super Mario Bros (Nintendo the creators of Super Mario Bros persuaded Great Giana Sisters maker Time Warp productions to remove the game for sale). The game has another classic soundtrack from Chris Hülsbeck - there are different soundtracks for each level. This game was a big hit with C64 users (especially those who hadn't played Super Mario) and earned 96% in Zzap!64 magazine.

There's not much in this game that you haven't seen in other platform games but the all round presentation and gameplay is more than sufficient to compensate for any sense of deja vu that players may carry over into the game. The backdriops have some welcome variety which help to freshen the game up periodically and prevent it from becoming too samey and the gameplay is fast, frantic, and addictive. The Great Giana Sisters basically takes all the best qualities of the platform game and deploys them within this very polished and fun platform adventure. The Great Giana Sisters is a game that platform lovers should have a blast with. This was one of those games that enjoyably gave you the slick console experience on the C64.

GREEN BERET (1986)

Label: Imagine, Designer: David Collier

Green Beret is a side scrolling shoot em up game. The player is an American soldier who has to free prisoners of war. There are four levels: missile, Harbour, Bridge and Prison Camp. At the end of each level is a "boss" who must be defeated. The player can jump, lay down and climb up ladders. After each 25000 points another life is given. Weapons include knife, flame thrower, bazooka or hand grenade. This is based on an arcade game released by Konami in 1985 and is a very good conversion. It is an action packed shooter with great graphics and atmospheric sound effects. The backgrounds and character animations are very good.

There is good range of enemies – soldiers, tanks, planes, which often come from both sides of the screen. There is also a classic soundtrack from Martin Galway. There are a range of fun enemies and weapons to use. One small drawback is that the game is quite difficult with lots of enemies - but it is still fun. To do well in the game one must learn to time and anticipate the proximity of enemies so you choose the precise moment to strike. This game is all action with the player constantly on the move and trying to make progress. This can definitely be a frustrating game but it's worth the effort if you like side-scrolling shooters. In North America this game is called Rush'n Attack.

Some players found Green Beret too tough to be completely satisfying but it all depends really on how good you are at these types of games and how willing you are to get better.

Green Beret is by no means original but it does have a polish and class that many similar games lack. The animations are

good and the music really drives the action. The sound effects
are very good too and are satisfying when you dispatch an
enemy. You start off the game with a knife but in the end you'll
have a generous arsenal at your disposal.

In this game you have to learn what weapons are best in given
situations. The knife is great to stick enemies as they run up to
you but if you want to clear your path in less constrictive
fashion you'll need something with more firepower. Because of
its difficulty, Green Beret was always something of an acquired
taste (some people never even got past the first level!) but it is
a terrific game of its type and was part of that exciting era
when C64 arcade conversions were becoming really good and
giving you something akin to an arcade experience at home.

HARDBALL! (1985)

Label: Accolade, Designer: Bob Whitehead

Hardball! is a baseball simulation. The game is shown behind
the pitcher and in a field view. Four 'pitch' types are shown
and chosen by joystick, followed by direction (e.g. low). When
fielding the player closest to the ball flashes and the joystick is
used to throw the ball in the required direction. For batting
there are four different types of shot, again chosen by the
joystick. The player chooses a team of ten from 25 players.
Their statistics and averages are shown. Even if you know
absolutely nothing about baseball, Hardball! is still easy to get
into and a blast once you start playing.

This is a great baseball game and was a very big seller. There
were quite a few good baseball games for the C64. Even as a
person who didn't have that much knowledge of baseball I
enjoyed the game. It would have been nice to see more great
cricket games on the C64 but American games companies were
naturally more interested in baseball sims! The gameplay in
Hardball! is very good with a range of options for batting and

pitching. You really feel like you are playing baseball and can play in different styles. There is a fielding element too. The graphics are colourful with big well animated players. This combines the arcade and simulation modes well with players with different abilities having an effect on the team. The team selection mode is a great addition.

Hardball! is a fantastic game for 1985 and one of the best sports simulations of that era. The animations are good and the ball has an authentic sense of weight and mass when it is struck. This game scores very highly in capturing the atmosphere of sport it is depicting and - all in all - it's difficult to know what more one might have asked for a 1985 baseball simulation. Hardball! ticks off all the boxes you'd want ticking in slick fashion and remains very playable. Trivia - Hardball! is the game that Fred Savage is playing in bed at the start of the cult 1987 film The Princess Bride.

If you like baseball games a game that is worth a look is 1987 Epyx game Street Sports Baseball. This game is somewhat different in that you have to select a baseball team from ordinary street kids and then take part in a game with them. Street Sports Baseball has the usual slick Epyx graphics and presentation and is quite good fun. The 1985 imagine game World Series Baseball is also pretty good - although less polished than Hardball! or Street Sports Baseball. Generally though, if you are looking for a baseball game, Hardball! is definitely the one to play above all others.

HEAD OVER HEELS (1987)

Label: Ocean, Designer: Jon Ritman and Bernie Drummond

Head Over Heels is an isometric arcade adventure and widely considered to be one of the great home computing games of the era. The player controls Headus Mouthion (Head) and Footus Underium (Heels) - two undercover agents from the planet Freedom. They are dispatched to Blacktooth to liberate the enslaved planets of Penitentiary, Safari, Book World and Egyptus. This game was originally on the Spectrum but the C64 version is equally as good. The graphics are crisp and detailed - though betraying their Spectrum origins (don't expect this to be the most amazing or colourful looking C64 game you've encountered) and the gameplay is absorbing.

Best of all Head Over Heels has a good flow to it. When you hear the words isometric arcade adventure you expect the game to be dreadfully slow but thankfully it isn't. What really makes this game special is the level design and feeling of exploration that the player experiences. This is no mean feat given the limited (by today's standards) tech of the era. This is a pretty challenging game but it is very addictive once you get into it and one of those games where you can't resist going back for another session. The designer Jon Ritman was heavily influenced by Knight Lore. He also said he wanted to make a game that made the player feel as if they were in a Disney cartoon (and a surreal one at that).

Head Over Heels earned a coveted Gold Medal award in ZZAP! 64 with an impressive 98% rating. This is one of those games that has lodged in people's memories and left them with fond impressions of this strange looking but very rewarding adventure game.

Head Over Heels is a perfect illustration of how one should never judge a book by its cover. Your first impression of this game, purely from a visual point of view, is unlikely to be ecstatic but once you begin playing the game the depth of gameplay and that amazing level design all comes to the fore. Head Over Heels is a great game on the whole and one that provided many addictive hours of gameplay to Spectrum and C64 users in the 1980s. The puzzles in this game should keep you going for quite some time.

H.E.R.O. (1984)

Label: The Softworks, Designer: John Van Ryzin

H.E.R.O. (standing for Helicopter Emergency Rescue Operation) was originally written for the Atari 2600 and is a pretty old game (even by C64 standards) but it has remained enduringly popular and usually gets a mention somewhere when anyone talks about the best or most memorable C64 games. The player takes on the part of the dashing Roderick Hero. Roderick is equipped with a Bond style backpack helicopter unit and must descend into the bowels of a mountain to rescue trapped miners. Here is the twist in the game to separate H.E.R.O. from your standard platform fare; the player is constantly going down rather than up.

Using the copter backpack you must hover down deeper and deeper. Obstacles have to be destroyed by dynamite to make progress possible and there are plenty of hazards like spiders and various unknown creatures who must be shot by Roderick's trusty laser weapon. This game comes from that era when it was all about high scores and points (as opposed to just finishing a campaign) and you score more and more points as you make progress and destroy all the monsters. While the gameplay is fairly simple it is very addictive and the game becomes more and more engrossing the further you get into it as the later levels are quite challenging and will force you to put your thinking cap on as you plot the best route down to the miners.

The graphics and sound in this game are nothing special at all but it doesn't really matter because H.E.R.O. is all about the gameplay and on this front it scores very highly indeed. H.E.R.O. is an amazingly simple but fun game with a great concept behind it and some inventive flourishes (I like the way the monsters come out of the water). This is very deserving of its status as a cult favourite.

HYPER SPORTS (1985)

Label: Imagine, Designer: David Collier

Hyper Sports is a multi-event sports game. It was originally an arcade game released by Konami. The sports are freestyle swimming, skeet shooting, pommel horse vaulting, archery, triple jump and weightlifting. This is a fun arcade multi-event sports game. It has a great sense of humour with the athlete often giving looks to the player and a range of fun music and sound effects. The sports are very playable too, although the swimming and weightlifting does involve some joystick waggling - which often ruined joysticks! Though not as polished as the Epyx sports simulations, Hyper Sports has plenty of character and is bags of fun with its eclectic range of sports.

The animations and graphics are somewhat cartoonish but not too silly and the events are pretty good fun individually. I always find the skeet shooting strangely absorbing and the swimming is a lot of fun too. The only event that is slightly disappointing is the archery because it has a fairly bland graphical presentation compared to the rest of the game. It's still quite good fun though and you have to contend with the prevailing winds to hit the arrows in the right spots. To be honest, Hyper Sports doesn't offer much that is tremendously new but it is a fun game in its own right and so proves to be a welcome addition to the endless glut of multi-sports simulations on the C64.

As long as your joystick can take the strain this game is very entertaining and one of my favourite sports games on the C64. There is an impressive amount of colour in the characters and backdrops and it's fun to master the individual sports on offer. You didn't really need too many more of these types of games after Epyx mastered the genre but if you have to find room for one more then Hyper Sports is worth a look. I can remember spending many enjoyable hours playing this game at the time.

If you are looking for something a bit different on the C64 when it comes to multi-event sports games you should definitely take a look at the 1988 Electronic Arts game

Caveman Ugh-Lympics. Caveman Ugh-Lympics is a comedy multi-event sports game. Set during the Stone Age there are six events. Saber Race - a foot race over obstacles while being chased by a sabre toothed tiger. Matetoss - a hammer style event but throwing the wife/husband. Fire making - a player races to make fire by rubbing stick together. Clubbing - two people have a club fight trying to club one another off a cliff edge. Dino Race - the player rides a dinosaur over an obstacle course. Dino vault - the player has to pole vault over a dinosaur, in this case a Tyrannosaurus rex. Six characters can be chosen from for the player to compete as. Each have their own specialities. The characters are Glunk: Clubbing, Saber Race. Crudla: Saber Race, Dino Vault. Thag: Matetoss, Fire Making. Ugha: Fire Making, Dino Race. Gronk: All disciplines! Vincent: None! Crudla is the only female character.

Caveman Ugh-Lympics is a fun and unusual sports game. There were numerous multi-event sports games on the C64. Many were based on real sports and others had more obscure or made up events. This one has a new twist being set in the Stone Age and having a Flintstones feel. The graphics are wonderful. Very colourful and cartoony with nicely animated and large characters. The events are varied and there is not a bad one among them - although there are only six. One thing that makes this game memorable is the humour with many comic touches and interesting things happening during the events. The opening ceremony makes fun of Epyx's Summer Games II opening ceremony.

Caveman Ugh-Lympics is a funny game - especially if you are using the two player mode. Caveman Ugh-Lympics offers amusing comic deflation of the pomp offered by the Epyx games and is generally just a great little game that offers a lot of offbeat fun. The only criticism one might make is that you feel like this game could have done with a couple more events just to prolong its playability somewhat. While the events you do get are enjoyable it feels as if something is slightly missing. This quibble aside though this is a fun cult game for the C64 and definitely worth a look if you like multi-sports games but have exhausted things like the Epyx series and Hyper Sports. Caveman Ugh-Lympics is basically Summer Games II meets The Flintstones and tremendous fun.

IMPOSSIBLE MISSION (1984)

Label: Epyx, Creator: Dennis Caswell

"Another visitor, stay awhile, stay forever!" In this classic platform game the player is a secret agent who must infiltrate the complex of Professor Elvin Atombender - who has been hacking computers vital to national security. The complex is made up of rooms with four levels accessible by lifts. Unfortunately for the spy they are defended by robots with a deadly electric ray weapon.

The player must search items in hidden in pieces of furniture and other items in different rooms to find puzzle pieces. The pieces must be put together to find a nine letter passcode for Atombender's control room so he can be stopped.

Caswell got the idea for Impossible Mission from the 1983 film War Games. War Games about a young computer hacker who hacks into an American supercomputer at NORAD (the North American Aerospace Defense Command) which is used to predict a nuclear war with the Soviet Union. Caswell was inspired by the supercomputer and wanted to create a game where someone has to battle in a computer controlled complex.

The game features an iconic piece of digitized speech at the start of the game. Caswell said the voice actor was "hammy" but the over the top aspect of the voice over was appropriate.

Impossible Mission is one of the most famous C64 games and anyone who played it at the time should have fond memories. It is strangely addictive manipulating the platforms so one can explore the rooms and avoid those pesky robots. The most striking thing about this game is the smooth animation of the character you play as he runs through corridors and somersaults over robots. This animation was very impressive indeed for the era.

Impossible Mission is a beautifully designed game in which the 'hub' (so to speak) is a lift which one must constantly return to in order to explore all the rooms in the underground complex. Using this lift and running through those corridors was satisfyingly atmospheric and gave one a sense of freedom and exploration that you usually didn't get in games like this at the time. Exploring the droid festooned rooms is also very addictive and will occasionally test your ability to solve platform puzzles.

The really great thing about Impossible Mission is that it felt like something completely new and fresh at the time - which was no mean feat given that this is essentially still very much a platform game. There was just something very stylish and legit about Mission Impossible which made it stand out from its peers and demand to be played.

Impossible Mission got a sequel in 1988 - although I gather the original creator wasn't involved. Impossible Mission II was not as famous as you might expect though and seems to have a mixed reputation these days. It could be that the sequel (unavoidably perhaps) simply didn't feel as fresh and novel as the original. Impossible Mission II gives you more of the same really (with a few graphical improvements) and is definitely worth playing if you like the first game.

All in all it is a solid enough sequel and the puzzles are tougher too (which might be a bonus or an annoyance depending on one's own personal taste).

INFILTRATOR (1986)

Label: US Gold, Designer Chris Gray

Infiltrator is a flight simulation/adventure game. In the game the player is Captain Jonny "Jimbo Baby" McGibbits - aka The Infiltrator. He has to fly the Wizbang Enterprises Gizmo'TM' DHX-1 attack helicopter. A mad scientist must be stopped. There are three mission each consisting of a flight sequence and a ground element. In the helicopter missions the player has to go to a landing area, engaging any enemy on the way. In the ground missions the player uses a number of items such as false papers and explosives to complete certain tasks. The player has to find a security card. This open security doors to achieve goals - such as neutralising nerve gas or rescuing an allied scientist.

Infiltrator is a fun adventure game in which the player pilots a super helicopter similar to the one from 80s action television series Airwolf. There are lots of different elements in the game – essentially a series of mini-games. The flight sim part and the base infiltration sequence could be separate games. The flight sim element is rather good for the C64 in 1986 although the graphics are a bit chunky. That was a very big deal at the time to see realistic hands controlling the helicopter! Infiltrator was definitely an ambitious sort of game with its blend of different styles and gameplay modes. It's to the credit of the game too that it all morphs together into a fairly satisfying unified game (as opposed to feeling like a bunch of underwhelming disconnected mini-games).

The part with the base infiltration is very well presented with different rooms having to be searched and some interesting tasks completed. The graphics are very colourful throughout the wide range of action screens, maps and mission report screens and there is a great sense of humour running through the game with the names of the characters and their depictions. Infiltrator creator Chris Gray also helped create the classic Boulderdash.

A sequel (Infiltrator 2) was made in 1988 - it is very similar to
the first and provides more gameplay in a similar vein for
Infiltrator fans. Be warned though, this game is no picnic
(learning to fly is pesky indeed) but it is a very immersive and
enjoyable experience for those who stick with it.

INTERNATIONAL BASKETBALL (1984)

Label: Commodore, Designer: Andrew Spencer

International Basketball is (naturally) basketball simulation.
Two teams of 3 players play over two 200 second periods. In
one player mode there are nine difficulty levels. NBA, Olympic
or NCAA rules can be chosen. This is a great early sports sim
from Andrew Spencer - who also wrote International Soccer.
The two games are very similar. The game is very playable
with a good depiction of basketball. Spencer improved on his
soccer game as the ball movement is more fluid. In
International Soccer the ball tended to be stuck to the floor on
occasion but here the ball can (obviously) be thrown about.
The graphics are attractive with quite big players and the
animations are good. There are a range of good sound effects
also in the game.

The weird thing about International Basketball and
International Soccer is that they can look slightly crude at first
glance and make you fear the worst for the game but then
when you actually play the game the gameplay is fantastic and
all your doubts are banished. The players in this game move at
what feels like the right speed. Not too slow (which would
obviously be highly frustrating!) but not too fast either.

The pace of the game means that you always feel in control
and have time to decide what to do with the ball. I have no
interest in the sport of basketball myself and never watch it

but I could happily play International Basketball for hours and it is very satisfying when you put together a fancy move and score some points. This is a great early sports sim for the C64 and highly recommended. International Basketball remains a pleasure to play. This is a really good game on the whole with plenty of colour and some nice background detail - which includes a clapping crowd and a ticking scoreboard.

Good basketball games were relatively thin on the ground when it comes to the C64 but one worth a mention is the Epyx game Street Sports Basketball - which is much in the vein of their Street Sports Baseball game. In the game you choose kids to take part in a three a side basketball match. I gather this was written by the same person who wrote International Basketball and you can see similarities in the animation and gameplay. The presentation is very slick (as one would expect from Epyx) and the game is fun. Whether it is different enough from International Basketball though is open to debate. I think it probably is.

The 1986 Activision game GBA Championship Basketball is probably worth a shout if you are desperate for more basketball action. This game is interesting in that you look down the court (as opposed to viewing the game from the side). GBA Championship Basketball is quite a realistic basketball game and has its admirers. I still think though that International Basketball is easily the king of basketball games on the C64.

INTERNATIONAL KARATE + (1987)

Label: System 3, Designer: Archer MacLean

International Karate + is a classic karate fighting game. In the game three karate fighters fight on a beach. The aim is to score six points. After two rounds there is a bonus game involving deflecting bouncing balls. One or two players can compete. IK

+ is arguably the best of the numerous martial arts games produced in the 80s for the C64. It has great animations and graphics and a classic score. The fighting is very good with a range of new moves. The three fighter aspect makes it different from games such as Way of the Exploding Fist. The bonus stage with the balls is a good addition.

This game only has one backdrop - the colours can be tweaked but a few more backdrops would have added some variety. One fun addition are Easter eggs. By using certain keystrokes a U-boat periscope, a pacman and spider appear. One keystroke drops the fighters trousers! The music is superb - a Merry Christmas, Mr Lawrence inspired piece by Rob Hubbard. In the US the game was called Chop N' Drop.

The game is a sequel to International Karate (1985) - which was what you might describe as a highly polished Exploding Fist clone. Many believe that IK+ is even better than the original (which is high praise) and that it is probably the best fighting game ever released on the C64. It is certainly a contender for that title with its smooth animations and excellent combat and gameplay. The computer AI here is tough enough to present a challenge to even the most adept player. There is apparently now a hacked version of this game in which you can take control of a third computer controlled power and so can enjoy some triple IK + carnage. International Karate + is a classic game of its type and very highly recommended.

KATAKIS (1988)

Label: Rainbow Arts, Designer: Manfred Trenz

Katakis is a horizontal scrolling shoot em up. In the game the player is on the planet of Katakis, an outer space human colony. Artificial Intelligence machines have been designed by scientists but they have evolved and taken over the planet. The humans are using DS-H75 space Eagle gliders to attack the AI machines and take back the planet. The ship can be upgraded with a satellite and different extra weapons by collecting balls or crystals. Enemy opponents must be killed on each level before taking on a larger end-boss at the end of the level. There are twelve levels

Katakis has a typically great soundtrack by Chris Hülsbeck to enjoy during the game. Each level has its own design. There are a few minor bugs but these do not tremendously detract from the game. The graphics are pleasing and the levels are different and well designed. There are a wide range of striking enemies and monsters in the game too. In the large range of C64 scrolling shoot em ups this is one of the best. The difficulty level is judged well too which helps the playability in these type of games.

The game is very similar to another shooter R-Type. R-Type was first released for the arcade in 1987. Activision Europe held the rights for R-Type conversions and said to the Katakis makers they could carry on selling Katakis if they made the Amiga conversion of R-Type. The Katakis programmer Manfred Trenz, graphic artist Andreas Escher and musician Chris Hülsbeck all worked on the C64 version of R-Type. In 1989 this game was re-released as Denaris.

If you like side scrolling blasters then Katakis should be right up your alley. The game is bright and attractive and the gameplay is challenging enough to keep one engaged.

There's an impressive amount of mayhem and detail on the screen and the colours of the backdrops change often enough to prevent the game from looking too samey and repetitive.

There were probably too many of these types of games on the C64 in the end but if you had to only sample a select few - the cream if you like - then Katakis would definitely be one of the distinguished games which went on that list.

KIKSTART II (1987)

Label: Mastertronic, Designer: Shaun Southern

Kikstart II is a dirt bike stunt motorcycling simulation. The game is side on and scrolls to the right. There is a split screen to view two players at one time. There are 24 courses plus a course designer to create new ones. A selection of 5 courses are raced on at one time. Obstacles include barrels, hedges, tables, gates, sand pits and eve flame throwers. Some obstacles can only be navigated at high or low speed. The bike can accelerate, decelerate, wheelie or jump.

This is a very simple looking but fun motorcycle racer and is very playable. The courses are well designed and the option to create more keeps the game fresh. There are humorous touches too - such as the flamethrower and various sound effects. The computer opponent is challenging and the two player option is fun.

There was also a first Kikstart game in 1985. The graphics were improved in this sequel but both games are equally good and worth playing. The amazing things about these games is that they were budget titles and only £1.99. Budget titles could be hit or miss sometimes but any C64 user of the era certainly got value for money with the Kikstart games.

The Kikstart games are the sort of games which don't look like much at first glance but prove to be immensely playable and addictive. One might argue that these are the best budget games ever released for the C64 - at the very least they are serious contenders for that crown. These two games offer a lot of fun and the icing on the cake is the course editor - a great addition for fans of this second game. Be warned though, if you do play Kikstart you won't get that theme music out of your head for days.

KUNG FU MASTER (1985)

Label: Data East, Designer: Numerous

Kung Fu Master is a side scrolling martial arts game. The player - Kung-Fu Master Thomas - is trying to rescue his girlfriend Sylvia who has been kidnapped by Mr X and is held in his Temple. Thomas must rescue Sylvia from the Temple fighting a number of different enemies over five levels of the temple.

This is a simple but very enjoyable fighting game. Although the graphics are nothing special they are effective. There are a number of mysterious enemies to fight - dwarves, giants, bees! One memorable aspect of the game is the catchy music played during the game. Dum diddy dum...

The game was originally a Japanese arcade game released in 1984 called Spartan X. The original game was designed by Takashi Nishiyama and inspired by Hong Kong martial arts films. The concept of a person fighting different enemies over different levels of a building came from the Bruce Lee film Game of Death. This is the film where Bruce wears the iconic yellow and black jumpsuit. Unfortunately, Bruce Lee died before the film was fully completed.

Kung Fu Master is probably not the sort of game you'll return to again and again once you have beaten it but you'll certainly play it to death at first as the game is very addictive with enjoyable fighting gameplay and a frantic pace. Kung Fu Master is a fun game of the whole and it always feels satisfying when you fight your way out of a level. This is not the most ambitious game on the C64 but what it sets out to do it does very well.

Anyone who was a fan of the arcade version would have been very happy with this C64 iteration of Kung Fu Master.

THE LAST NINJA 2 (1988)

Label: System 3, Designer: John Twiddy

The Last Ninja 2 is an adventure/3D arcade game. The player plays a Ninja who is in New York attempting to defeat his enemy Kunitoki. He must fight through several levels fighting opponents and picking up objects such as keys and maps which are needed to finish the game. This is a sequel to 1987 game The Last Ninja. Although the isometric screens have to be loaded individually (which is rather frustrating to say the least) the game looks great - taking the C64 graphics capability to the limit. The puzzles are interesting and the combat is very good. Matt Gray also produced a classic soundtrack for the game.

The Last Ninja 2 does still share one annoying part in the first game with some annoying jumps that have to be executed perfectly - although the jumps are slightly easier here. The game was a big success and sold 5 million copies - meaning 1 in 4 C64 owners bought the game. Although the first game was very well received most trade publications and gamers of the era felt that this sequel was even better - mostly thanks to improved gameplay. The Last Ninja games were very state of the art for the era and a big deal at the time. These games were considered to be hugely ambitious and stretched what was thought capable on the C64.

What these games did really well was to incorporate the beat em up into a broader game that involved puzzles and exploration. This was all fairly new at the time as fighting games basically tended to limit the player to a single screen. While the combat in Last Ninja is not as satisfying as something like Exploding Fist you do get a huge new game on top of the fighting though and the exploration offered and world building is very impressive. There was later a third game in the Last Ninja series and it received reviews pretty much in line wit the previous games. All the Last Ninja games are

worth playing and this series is rightfully considered to be a
classic of the C64 era.

LASER SQUAD (1989)

Label: Blade Software, Designer: Julian Gollop

Laser Squad is an enduring cult favourite on the C64 and was
essentially the blueprint for the famous MSDOS game X-COM:
UFO Defense. Julian Gollop designed both Laser Squad and
X-Com. X-Com was even originally conceived as a Laser Squad
sequel. You can definitely see the seeds of X-Com in this game.
Laser Squad is a tactics and strategy based game in which you
have to control a team to perform various objectives. You'll
have to keep your team healthy and stocked up with weapons
as you guide them the game's map.

There are various scenarios and the game has something of an
outlandish sci-fi tint (which is fun and stops it from becoming
another dry and serious military simulation). Laser Squad, as
befitting a game which is essentially X-Com before X-Com, is a
very absorbing game to play once you get into it and the depth
to the gameplay and the world the game creates is impressive
on both counts.

The graphics for the above view perspective are nothing to
write home about but there are some excellent particle and
strobe effects which give the game an enjoyably trippy quality
at times. The design of the game means that everything is easy
to follow and see and you do become genuinely absorbed in
the tasks involving your team. You also become engrossed in
the challenges of keeping your team alive and healthy. The
shoot outs in the game are good fun and there are various
weapons to use.

This game is probably more fun as a playing experience than
most 'straight' military simulations so it has a lot of appeal for

those who enjoy strategy games but don't wnt to get too bogged down with details and a user manual the size of a telephone directory.

Laser Squad is an intelligent and very playable strategy game and the two player mode is especially fun. If you do get into this game expect to lose many hours of your life playing it. Even if you've only encountered the X-Com games and have no idea what Laser squad is you should take a look at this to see where it all started. Because of the depth of gameplay,

Laser Squad has good replay value and keep you going for a long time. This is one of the cleverest games released on the C64 and a very good one too.

LAW OF THE WEST (1985)

Label: Accolade, Designer: Alan Miller

Law of the West is a western themed adventure game with selectable answers. The player is the sheriff of Gold Gulch, a small wild west town. The player has a conversation with the gunslingers and various characters such as the doctor, women, fellow lawmen and a gambler, choosing from four answers each time. The different answers create different plot lines.

If there is a shoot out a cursor appears to show the direction of the players bullet. If the sheriff is shot he must be helped by the doctor. The doctor will help or leave the sheriff for dead depending on the sheriff's previous conversations with him.

There are four locations: The Saloon, The Wells Fargo stagecoach office, The train station, The bank. The game ends when the sheriff is shot or the conversations with the eleven characters end. The final score is calculated from crimes prevented - how the characters were dealt with and interactions with the lady characters.

This is a fun atmospheric wild west game. The graphic backgrounds are great for the C64 and very colourful and the animations and depictions of the other characters are very good. The sound effects add to the game too - such as the galloping of the horses. There is a good plot which changes according to the answers chosen. For each conversation with a character there are three conversation phases with four answers leaving 64 possible endings to each conversation. You can be diplomatic, or just insult the characters and then shoot them. The shooting scenes mean this is an early 3D shooter.

The replay value of Law of the West is probably questionable after you've exhausted the question and answer possibilities but - although not considered a classic at the time - this is an inventive and interesting game that's sort of like a more basic forerunner to later more elaborate and polished adventure games like Monkey Island.

Law of the West is a fun attempt to make a slightly different type of western game and although the plot and gameplay could have done with more depth this is a likeable game that is well worth experiencing if you like the sound of it.

Another western themed game (though very different from Law of the West) I would recommend is 1984's High Noon by Ocean Software. High Noon is a western shoot em up. The player is a sheriff who must defend the town against various outlaws. The game has 5 levels, which get progressively more difficult. After the completion of each level, there is a duel between the sheriff and an outlaw. If the levels are completed the game starts again.

This is a very simple early C64 game which is nevertheless great fun and highly addictive. There are a number of fun touches such as an undertaker who gets rid of the bodies. Jaunty music from the 1952 western film High Noon adds to the fun. This game was only released on the C64 and is well worth a play.

LEADER BOARD (1986)

Label: Access Software, Creators: Bruce Carver, Roger Carver

Leader Board is a golf simulation and was a huge hit in 1986. There are four courses with the usual 18 holes per round. Up to 4 players can compete. There are three difficulty settings: Novice, Amateur and Professional. In professional there is wind which effects the ball. To play a shot the player has to choose a club and put a cursor in the direction the ball is to be hit, then press fire when the desired power on a bar is reached and again when the required amount of snap is reached. To putt, there is a stick with a shadow line indicating the slope of the green. Hold the fire button down and let go and when the required amount of power in the power bar is reached to make a putt.

In the original game the courses had only grass and water. Leader Board Executive was released in 1987 and features bunkers and trees. Leader Board Executive has a sort of brown desert type surface outside the green of the course. The third edition of the game was World Class Leader Board which featured real life courses. My personal favourite is Leader Board Executive as I enjoy the look and atmosphere of the courses.

Golf games can be a bit slow and overly complex (working out how to actually hit the ball can even be a palava in some of the more annoying golf games!) but Leader Board is easy to get into and simple to play. You don't even have to be a fan of golf to enjoy this game. Bruce Carver created the game. He was responsible for classic games such the Beach Head I and II and Raid Over Moscow. He later created another iconic golf game - Links. Leader Board is designed perfectly and simply and the controls make it a pleasure to play. One might argue that this is one of the greatest games ever released on the C64. Right away you knew you were in the presence of a very special game.

There is something very satisfying and relaxing about playing Leader Board. The flight of the ball is perfect and because you aren't harassed with endless complications concerning the intricate minutiae of golf you can just start playing straight away. Later golf games might look better than Leader Board but none of them have ever been so simple and pleasurable to play. Leader Board is a true masterpiece of the C64 era and a must play game. Even if you find real golf boring you will definitely still enjoy playing Leader Board.

LITTLE COMPUTER PEOPLE (1985)

Label: Activision, Designer: David Crane

Little Computer People is a social simulation game. In the game the player interacts with a character in a house and looks after him. The screen shows a three story house with no wall and various rooms. The rooms are Den, study, Bedroom, Bathroom, Office, kitchen and living room. In it the character goes about his routine - doing activities such as reading, cooking and watching television. The player interacts with this character by entering commands for the character to perform actions such as reading the newspaper.

Sometimes the character asks the player to do an activity with him such as playing a game of poker. The character has to be cared for by the player and made happy. Food and drinks must be provided. Each time a new game is started a unique character is created for the players copy of the game. The name of the character is chosen randomly from list of 256 names.

Little Computer People is a fun and ground-breaking game for 1985. It is very pleasant to play spending time with the character and his dog. The graphics are very cosy and the characters are charmingly animated. There are great sound effects and a range of musical tunes - including Jingle Bells at Christmas. One nice aspects was that the programmers created unique characters on the different disks.

The designer David Crane said - "An interesting thing about the program, and what most of the buyers didn't notice, is that it has been duplicated within the company. Since we had control over each disc, we gave every copy of the game its own unique serial number. This number was then used to generate the personality, appearance and behaviour of the Little Computer person on this disc. Based on the serial number, the following was determined: name, shirt color, personality characteristics, etc. These were determined independently, probably a lot of serial numbers generated a computer person named Tom, but the chance that two of these also had the same color of shirt was almost zero. Each disc was effectively unique."

Little Computer People rather anticipates The Sims series. The Sims creator Will Wright said he played Little Computer People when it was first released. When he was developing The Sims, Wright said he got some good feedback from Little Computer People's designers. The disk version had many more features than the tape version. Little Computer People is a unique game way ahead of its time. This was a wonderful experience for C64 owners who were looking for something a bit different.

By the way, if you are looking for something else a bit different on the C64 you might want to check out 1986 Activision game Alter Ego. This is a text game in which you basically make decisions for an imaginary person and live their life. The decisions you make right from childhood will determine what that life turns out to be like.

Alter Ego (which came in both male and female versions) is a hard game to describe but it is very addictive and a genius piece of software. The game got 98% in ZZAP!64 and is very highly regarded by those who played it back in the eighties. You should definitely take a look at Alter Ego if you take the time to explore the C64 era.

LODE RUNNER (1983)

Label: Broderbund, Designer: Doug Smith

Lode Runner is a classic platform game in which the player controls a little figure (who is supposed to be a Galactic Commando battling the corrupt and evil Bungeling Empire) who must collect all the gold in each level before climbing to the top. You can dig holes to trap the enemy guards (and conveniently walk over them!) and must make strategic use of ladders to navigate each level and climb to the top. You start the game with five lives and get an extra life each time you complete a level. Lode Runner is quite simply a brilliant blending of a puzzler, platform game, and arcade action.

This game was hugely successful and sold many copies in the months and years after its release. The creator of Tetris even name checked Lode Runner as his favourite puzzle game. Although this is ostensibly a platform game (and a fun platform game too) strategy is required to complete the various levels so not only is the gameplay wonderfully addictive but you'll also need your thinking cap at times to deduce the best way to complete a level.

The graphics in this game are rather basic (the backdrops have a brick motif) and the sound amounts to little more than sonic beeps but it doesn't matter in the slightest because the gameplay is so fantastic. That said though, the animations of the stick figures are pretty good for the time. There are 150 screens in Lode Runner so you can't complain about lack of content. This game should keep you going for some time.

One excellent (and rather ahead of its time) feature in Lode

Runner is that the game offered a DIY screen generator editor in which you could design and edit your own levels. That was a pretty new concept in 1983. The makers of the game even ran a competition to see which player could design the best screen. By the way, the cover art for Lode Runner, a sort of cartoon sci-fi Logan's Run (ish) type illustration, was really good. Lode Runner is a well thought out and exceptionally playable piece of vintage game design and more than worthy of its hallowed reputation. Lode Runner was so popular it even got an arcade conversion. Usually it was the other way around!

MANIAC MANSION (1987)

Label: Lucasfilm Games, Designer: Ron Gilbert, David Fox, Carl Mey

Maniac Mansion is a point and click graphic adventure game. The player is Dave Miller - who is trying to rescue his girlfriend Sandy Pantz from a mad scientist called Dr Fred Evison. Dr Evison is holding Sandy in his mansion. The player chooses two characters from six to assist Dave Miller: Bernard, Jeff, Michael, Razor, Syd and Wendy. Each of these six characters have their own personality and skills to help solve the puzzles. The game has five endings - depending on which characters are selected. The characters are controlled by clicking on action words (i.e. walk, unlock) in a text area using a cursor. The game ends when all three members and Sandy have been guided to safety.

This is an iconic game and was Lucasfilm Games first published game. Creator Ron Gilbert wanted something different from the simple written text commands of adventure games so created a new system. It was a point and click method where action words were clicked on with a cursor. He created a game engine called SCUMM which was used in other Lucasfilm games such as Monkey Island. One of the nice things about this game is that it is quite non-linear. There is

more than way to beat the game so you don't have to do the
same things all the time. Sometimes it actually pays dividends
to try something different.

Maniac Mansion is fun to play and very humorous. It has a
great horror film story (and patently inspired by The Rocky
Horror Picture Show) and memorable characters. The story
was based on cliches from horror films such as Friday the 13th
and A Nightmare on Elm Street. The multiple endings and
interactive story make it very playable. Maniac Mansion was a
tremendous breath of fresh air in 1987 and made the humble
arcade adventure suddenly feel more complex, fun, ambitious,
and cinematic. This set a high bar for Lucasfilm games to come
but it was a challenge they frequently seemed to meet with
flying colours.

MANIC MINER (1983)

Label: Software Projects, Designer: Matthew Smith

A classic Spectrum platform game, the C64 version of Manic
Miner was good enough to earn 95% in ZZAP!64. Though this
game looks downright primitive to modern eyes this is
addictive platform fun and an ingenious game of its type. In
the game the player is Miner Willy - who while out prospecting
stumbles into the evidence of a superior lost civilisation. The
enemies include robots and spiders and - as with most
platform games - you'll have to make shrewd use of the
platforms to navigate your way through the screens and onto
the next part.

The graphics are nothing special and many people think the
music in this game is annoying but for pure history alone this
game deserves a mention on any list of classic C64 games. The
collusion detection in this game is not perfect (which can
obviously lead to frustration at times) but the gameplay itself
is excellent and should please any fans of platform games or

just vintage games in general. For a number of C64 owners this is the first game they remember playing so it has a special nostalgic appeal for this reason lone. Most people seem to think the Spectrum version was better but it's a minor quibble because the C64 iteration of Manic Miner is pretty damn good too.

Manic Miner is a trip way back to the early years of the C64 - where these types of games were already becoming fairly common. Manic Miner stood out from the pack though because of the timeless gameplay and enjoyable atmosphere of retro goodness. This is far from the most ambitious game ever put out on the C64 but for the pure hours of fun it supplied, Manic Miner was tremendous value for money and terrific stuff. This is one of those C64 games that looks hopelessly dated today but the average visual presentation shouldn't put you off from sampling a likeable dose of C64 history.

MIDNIGHT RESISTANCE (1990)

Label: Ocean, Designer: Robert W. Rinman

Midnight Resistance is a side scrolling shoot em up. Set in a dystopian future, the player is a resistance fighter who is on a mission to rescue his family from a drug boss. The player has to fight soldiers, jets and tanks in the game. When enemies are killed they give red keys to the player which are used to buy extra weapons. There are nine levels. 6 red keys by the 8th level are needed to free all family members. This is a great shot em up. The player controls a Rambo type character. There are lots of weapons and enemies to fight. One nice aspect is the ability to shoot in all directions. The scrolling is smooth and the graphics are very good. The levels are different which adds variety. There is a great soundtrack too.

The game was first released in 1989 as a Japanese arcade game called Middonaito Rejisutansu. Trivia - the arcade game was so popular it had a cameo in the film Robocop 2. You've probably played a lot of these Metal Slug style games but Midnight Resistance was definitely a cut above the others. The game looks terrific and the gameplay is responsive and satisfying. The opening stages lull you in and then the carnage cranks up the more you progress. This is one of the best arcade conversions of the C64 era and even if you were familiar with the arcade machine you couldn't fail to be impressed by this C64 version.

Midnight Resistance is bags of fun and a fantastic side scrolling action game. The running, jumping, and shooting is all great fun and the diverse variety of colourful and ever changing backdrops serves as a nice way to constantly freshen the game up in a visual sense and stop it from ever appearing too samey. Midnight Resistance is classic stuff. The only real shame is the lack of a two player mode. There was an Amiga version of this too but the C64 version is arguably still the best.

MICROPOSE SOCCER (1988)

Label: MicroProse Software, Designer: Chris Yates

Micropose Soccer is a football game. It has a top down view. There is the usual eleven a side game but also included is a 6 a side indoor mode. There are a number of international teams and players can choose to compete in a World cup tournament, a league, or a friendly with two teams. This is a great football sim which vies with Emlyn Hughes for the title of best C64 football game. It depends on what you prefer - top down or side on.

The game was inspired by the arcade game Tehkan World Cup. It is extremely playable with instinctive controls and includes shots such as overhead kicks and banana shots. One fun feature is an action replay which simulates a tape rewinding before showing the replay. Another nice feature is different weather - including rain. The game was developed by Jon Hare and Chris Yates of Sensible Software. They later created the Amiga classic Sensible Soccer - which was obviously inspired by Microprose Soccer. Sensible Soccer is an all time classic too.

There were endless football games on the C64 and many of them were terrible (if memory serves, Peter Beardsley's International Football was the absolute nadir when it came to the glut of soccer games) but football fans were more than well catered for with the arrival of Emlyn Hughes and Micropose Soccer. I personally prefer Emlyn Hughes because it feels like more of a 'straight' football simulation whereas Micropose Soccer is more of an arcade experience but both are really good and you should certainly play them both.

Micropose Soccer ((ahem) scores most heavily in its ability to create lots of action and a fast pace to the game. You'll definitely got caught up in the match when you ply this. If you want to see the game which layed down the blueprint for Sensible Soccer then you should make sure you play the classic Micropose Soccer. This is definitely one of the best football games ever made for the C64 and that's high praise because there were millions of them!

On the subject of football games, though many of them were awful I should give a mention to the Epyx game Street Sports Soccer - yet another entry in their Street Sports series.

Street Sports Soccer basically has you choosing kids for a game of three a side football in the park. Though it isn't a realistic football sim it is very playable and decent fun. Outside of Emlyn Hughes and Micropose Soccer, Street Sports Soccer is definitely one of the better football themed games.

I'm afraid I can't say the same for Ocean's 1987 game Match Day II - which inexplicably got 90% in ZZAP!64. Match Day II is simply too slow for my tastes. It's as if the players in Match Day II are playing football underwater! You should of course not forget International Soccer - which is excellent and up there with Emlyn Hughes and Micropose Soccer.

MONTEZUMA'S REVENGE (1984)

Label: Parker Bros, Designer: Robert Jaegar

Montezuma's Revenge is a platform game. The player is Panama Joe, a person moving around the 16th Century Aztec temple of Aztec Emperor Montezuma II. He jumps, runs and climbs poles, chains and ladders. There are obstacles, traps and enemies to contend with. Jewels must be collected and enemies killed. Obstacles include conveyor belts, fire pits,, disappearing floors and laser gates. Enemies include skulls, snakes and spiders. Panama Joe uses equipment such as swords, amulets and torches and only a certain number of objects can be carried at one time. There are 10 floors in the Pyramid with 99 rooms. The aim is to reach the Treasure Chamber on the bottom level.

Montezuma's Revenge is a fun early jump and run platform game with the simple graphics of the era. The Aztec setting is fun and the Panama Joe character is animated nicely. The action is inventive and fast paced with well laid out rooms and this game should keep you going for a while. These types of games if executed correctly are always addictive. 16 year old Robert Jaegar originally came up with the game for the Atari 800.

There isn't an intricate amount of detail in the backdrops and animations but the characters are colourful and charmingly bulky and there is at least plenty of colour to offset the fact that - graphically - this isn't the most elaborate game in the world. You'll be doing all the usual stuff in this game like climbing ladders, jumping onto ropes, and navigating platforms to reach a set goal. There is nothing tremendously new here but for some reason Montezuma's Revenge is tremendously addictive and likeable and must rank close to the top table when it comes to platform games on the C64. This is an oldie but a goodie.

MONTY ON THE RUN (1985)

Label: Gremlin Graphics, Designer: Jason Perkins

This is the third game in the Monty Mole series. The plot (such as it is) has Monty on the (you guessed it) run and heading for the English channel. Naturally this means there will be, as per usual, plenty of platform capers and puzzles to solve. Even way back in 1985 gamers could probably be forgiven for wondering if the world really needed yet another platform game but Monty on the Run manages to justify its own existence with fast paced action and plenty of surreal flourishes. Even if you were rather jaded by the platform genre by now, Monty on the Run is still a pleasure to play and a fun experience.

This is one of those platform games that moves pretty fast so the player is always engaged and focused on the puzzle (and indeed pitfall) at hand and facing our hero Monty. You can climb ropes and jump and look out for those pesky pistons - which will crush our hero if you don't time your progress right. Deadly obstacles include (for some reason) water - which Monty is most definitely not a fan of.

Where this game scores highly is the surreal aura which permeates the action. The enemies include things like gloved hands and what look like steaming teapots. The weirdness and humour in the game is often a delight and makes the action and platform antics even more enjoyable. The enemies all have plenty of character and the game is so weird you find yourself taking in all the background detail and just enjoying all the strangeness of it all. These enjoyable flourishes help to mitigate the fact that in terms of graphics this isn't the most astounding looking game you'll ever see on the C64.

Monty on the Run is tremendous fun on the whole and a great platformer with some inventive touches and plenty of offbeat charm and character. The music is great and the game is entertaining to play. Even if you were sick of platform games this was definitely one of those games to make an exception for and enjoy.

THE MOVIE MONSTER GAME (1986)

Label: Epyx, Designer: Numerous

In this game the player is one of five monsters rampaging through a city. The monsters are Godzilla, Sphectra – a wasp, The Glog – a blob, a giant spider called Tarantus, Mr Meringue - a version of the Stay Puff Marshmallow Man from the Ghostbusters film, and a Transformers style robot called Mechatron. Cities included are New York, San Francisco, London, Tokyo, Moscow and Paris. There are five scenarios: Beserk: destroy as many buildings and vehicles. Escape: escape the city before being killed. Search: rescue a relative of the monster. Destroy Landmark: destroy a landmark in a city. Lunch: eat vehicles and civilians.

This is a fun game based on monsters from various classic horror films. The game is nicely presented in typical Epyx fashion which adds to the atmosphere and fun of the game. At the start a cinema is shown where the "movie" to play can be chosen. In the cinema the show starts with an advertisement and then the feature presentation starts – which is the game itself. There is a good selection of monsters and scenarios. The graphics are very appealing. This is a fantastic idea for a game and although it isn't a perfect game the concept at the heart of the game is sufficient of itself to mitigate some of the flaws.

The main criticism of this game is that it's rather slow. The monsters don't move very fast and you won't get arcade speed carnage here. This was clearly disappointing for a lot of gamers and reviewers because The Movie Monster Game got fairly lukewarm reviews when it was released. Many reviewers seemed to feel that once you'd played this a few times it didn't have great replay value or the sort of gameplay that would constantly draw you back to the game. Personally though I had a soft spot for this game because of the monster concept. Who wouldn't want to play Godzilla and destroy a city in a game?

While the actual game was never going to be as amazing as the concept it does have a great atmosphere, many nice touches, and it is definitely an experience of the like you had never seen on the C64 before. One might argue that this game is a trifle too ambitious for the tech of the era but if you lower your expectations somewhat then this is still a solid and attractively presented and designed game which doubtless fascinated monster mad C64 kids in the 1980s. While this game may or may not have a tremendously high replay value over time it is worth a look and highly inventive. Trivia - Epyx managed to licence the use of Godzilla in the game.

NEBULUS (1987)

Label: Hewson Consultants, Designer: John M. Phillips

Nebulus is a platform game. In the game the player is a green creature named Pogo. Eight towers that have been built in the sea have to be destroyed by planting bombs in them. Each tower is played in turn and the player goes from the bottom to the top. The towers are shaped like a cylinder and have ledges on the outside of them with stairs and elevators. Enemies must be shot. Pogo can be knocked off the tower and killed. At the top of each tower is a destruction mechanism which is triggered. Pogo then enters a submarine and has a bonus having to catch fish in the submarine.

This is a fun, addictive platform game with nice cartoony

graphics. The characters are nicely animated and the parallax scrolling where the tower rotates as Pogo wakes around it is very impressive. The bonus game with the submarine is great too and features some very nice scrolling. It is perhaps a little too challenging but the puzzles and game play are great fun. Though the game is frustrating you will still keep coming back to play again and again!

By the time that Nebulus came out, the C64 already had more platform games than any one person could ever possibly hope to play. There was definitely room for one more though because this game was a tremendous success and managed to bring some freshness to this well trodden game genre. The navigation of the rotating towers was rather novel and felt like something different from the usual platform shenanigans. This game felt like a true arcade experience - only at home rather than the seaside arcade.

Most of us probably feel like we've played too many platform games but Nebulus is inventive enough to be worth making an exception for. This is an attractive and very playable game with a winningly strange atmosphere.

ON COURT TENNIS (1984)

Label: Activision, Designer: Michael J. Archer

On Court Tennis is (obviously) a tennis simulation. Clay, hard or grass court can chosen (although the court is always green). One or two player options are available. One set, best of 3 or best of 5 sets can be played.

There are a number of good tennis sims for the C64. These include International Tennis (Commodore 1985), Pro Tennis Tour (1989 Ubisoft) and International Tennis (1992 Zepplin Games). On Court Tennis is however my own personal favourite. The graphics are rudimentary but it is extremely playable. The player automatically moves into position during play but there are a good range of shots which makes the game very playable.

You can have some great rallies in this game and play some satisfying shots. The computer opponents are competitive and it is great in two player mode. Maybe the option to change the hair and clothing colour of the characters or name them would have been good though. You can only choose to be Bjorn, Jimmy, John or Ivan (named after the tennis players Bjorn Borg, Jimmy Connors, John McEnroe and Ivan Lendl).

Tennis games (rather like the sport they are based on) can easily be frustrating if the gameplay isn't right but On Court Tennis manages to avoid this pitfall and is very enjoyable and playable. If you could only pick one tennis game on the C64 this is probably the one to go for. Other games worth a look are Match Point and 1990's Great Courts. For my money though On Court Tennis was never quite surpassed when it comes to C64 tennis sims. This is a great sports sim on the whole and a lot of fun.

OPERATION WOLF (1988)

Label: Ocean, Designer: Colin Porch

Operation Wolf is a shoot em up game - essentially a rail shooter. These sorts of games were popular before advances in tech paved for the way for the era of the FPS (which truly began with games like Wolfenstein and Doom and soon became the most popular genre in gaming). The player in Operation Wolf has to shoot enemies in the form of soldiers, tanks and helicopters aiming with a cross hair. Ammunition can be gained by shooting at ammo in the game. The aim is to free captives. There are 6 levels: concentration camp; powder magazine, communication setup; airport; village and Jungle.

This is a great version of the popular arcade game. It is one of the initial first person shooter style games, a genre that is of course still extremely popular today. Naturally this has great C64 graphics and music. The gameplay is fantastic too and very addictive - it is wonderful for a game of its type on the C64. It has been argued that playing Operation Wolf with a joystick is quite difficult. The option to use a mouse was available on the game. I personally had no major problems with joystick control.

Operation Wolf is quite violent - which drew complaints at the time of release. This controversy seems rather tame from a modern vantage point because modern games are often incredibly violent without kicking up a major fuss (though of course computer games have introduced a ratings system since the days of Operation Wolf). Anyone who enjoyed Operation Wolf in the arcades could have few complaints about this C64 conversion - which is fast, frenetic, colourful, and violent. Operation Wolf offers plenty of fast shooting Rambo style action fun and is highly recommended.

A 1990 sequel to this game was titled Operation Thunderbolt. The general perception seems to be that this sequel is competent but not quite as playable or fresh as the original. The sequel got 92% in ZZAP!64 but other magazines were more critical and felt this sequel wasn't as good. You should probably take a look at Operation Thunderbolt if you've played the first game but the original is definitely the one to seek out first.

PARADROID (1985)

Label: Hewson Consultants Ltd, Designer: Andrew Braybrook

Paradroid is a top down shoot em up/puzzle game. Enemy forces have taken over robots on spaceships and turned them against the crew. The player controls a robot that can take control of the other robots. There are 24 robots of 10 classes which have numbers on them: the higher the numbers the more powerful the droid is. Different droids have different power - such as speed and weaponry. Robots can be killed with a weapon and can be taken over by linking with them. This takes place in a mini-game where power must be supplied to different circuits. If the player takes over a droid, he can only use it for a certain level of time before the droid self destructs and the player reverts back to his original basic droid.

The spaceship has 16 decks with numerous rooms and 400 screens. The decks and rooms are connected by elevators and doors. Computer terminals can be accessed to provide maps and information on the droids. When one ship is cleared the player is beamed onto another. On beating the eight ship the player starts that ship again with tougher droids to face.

Paradroid is a classic game. It may look relatively simply graphically (sort of like Pac-Man) but it is a very addictive game. The scrolling is extremely smooth, with very good controls and it is great fun to control the different droids with their different weapons, speed etc. The effects - such as flashes look very good.

There is variety in the decks with different colours. The sound effects add to the atmosphere. Programmer Andrew Braybrook also created the classic shoot em up Uridium. Though this is not the most amazing looking game you've ever seen it does have bags of atmosphere and there is just something compelling about the aura of this game with its electronic sonic backdrop and addictive gameplay. Paradroid is an example of how a game doesn't necessarily need fancy graphics or obtuse concepts to be great.

There is a clarity of purpose in Paradroid that makes it all come together incredibly well. You get the happy sense here that Andrew Braybrook not only knew exactly what he was going for and wanted to do but actually achieved this with flying colours. Paradroid is one of those that still features near the top of lists concerning the best C64 games. It is more that worthy of that lofty reputation.

PITSTOP II (1984)

Label: Epyx, Designer: Stephen H. Landrum with Dennis Caswell

Pitstop II - as the name suggests - is a racing game. The player competes in races in six circuits: Brands Hatch, Hockenheim, Rouen-Les-Essarts, Sebring, Vallelunga, and Watkins Glen. Three (six of nine laps) races can be chosen. There are three difficulty levels. Players have to refuel and change tires in a pitstop. The players control the refuelling and the changing of the tires. The game is split screen with two views of the track with two cars view of the race; the two cars race each other. A single race can be chosen, or a season of races can be played.

This an early C64 racing game with a then revolutionary split-screen mode. It has smooth scrolling and a good pitstop feature where the player can be the mechanics repairing the car and adding fuel. This pitstop feature provides a strategic element. A nice touch is that markings on the wheel of the car indicate when a pitstop is needed. The graphics are good for the time. The computer opponents are good too with the computer cars having their own personality. A season of races is available which adds to the fun. The game comes into its own in the two player mode. Impossible Mission creator Dennis Caswell did the pitstop section. Pitstop II is a considerable improvement over the 1983 original. By the way, the cover art for the box is terrific too.

There are a number of good racing games for the C64. One game that is definitely worth playing and deserving of a spot in this book is 1991's Turbo Charge by system 3. The blurb for

Turbo Charge goes like this - 'Terrorists have broken into a UN ammo stockpile and stolen enough missiles to wipe a small country off the face of the earth! It's up to you, as Agents Agaippa and Drusus, to chase after the haul and reclaim it. But you'll have to be on your guard because it's difficult enough to navigate through roads at the best of times without having to worry about the mines and choppers that are being put in your way to slow you down!'

Turbo Charge, as the blurb suggests, is a lot of fun. There are a huge variety of enemy cars and you'll Engel in shoot outs as you try to force them off the road. There are tanker trucks, helicopters, and a number of different backdrops in which the action takes place. The graphics are a trifle blocky but get the job done and Turbo Charge is always as fast and furious as you'd want a racing game to be. This game is great fun.

Also worth a look is Power drift - a Japanese kart racing arcade game which got a C64 conversion. Power Drift is graphically quite similar to Turbo Charge though more cartoonish in approach. Like Turbo Charge though, Power Drift is fast and fun racing action and highly recommended if you like driving games.

For pure nostalgia reasons, I would also include 1984's Pole Position in any list of C64 racing games. Pole Position is a conversion of the Namco arcade classic, distributed by Atari outside Japan.

This was one of the first racing games I can recall being aware of and although the graphics are a trifle blocky and Pole Position was soon surpassed by other C64 racing games I had an awful lot of fun with Pole Position as a kid and played it for hours on end. You wouldn't say that Pole Position was a classic game (even within its own prescribed genre) but it provide me with a lot of fun and that's basically what computer games are all about aren't they?

PLATOON (1987)

Label: Ocean Software, Designer: Zach Townsend

Platoon is a shoot em up/action game. It is an adaption of the 1986 Oliver Stone Vietnam war film Platoon. There are three levels from a different perspective.

In the first level - a side scrolling section - the player guides a platoon of five men through the jungle. An explosive device must be found and used to demolish a bridge. Then a village needs to be searched and a secret tunnel of the Vietcong found. In the second section, with a first person view, the player is exploring the tunnel searching for a compass and a flare and shooting Vietcong soldiers. When leaving the tunnel the player has to fight a Vietcong attack. The third level sees the player having to kill a renegade US Sergeant Barnes and find shelter within two minutes.

Platoon is a very good licenced game (though, for entertainment purposes, it has more in common with Rambo than the Oscar nominated film it is based on). Many licenced games for the C64 were terrible but this is one of the better ones. There are a variety of mini-games which is a great idea rather than offering up the usual side scrolling platform themed film adaption. The second level is an early first person shooter and quite well executed. It's basically an Operation Wolf style section - which comes as a nice surprise because you sort of assume the jungle section at the start is going to be the whole game.

Games that are composed of diverse mini-games run a risk in that if the mini-games are individually unsatisfying they are unlikely to create a classic overall game but Platoon's mini sections are all diverting and actually blend together quite well into a larger unified game. The last section was felt to be a trifle frustrating by some gamers but - generally - this game all hangs together pretty well and is an interesting and entertaining experience. The graphics are very good and there is a great soundtrack which adds to the effectiveness of the Platoon adaption. Platoon's greatest strength though is in the variety of game styles it offers. This means that the game never feels too samey and always throws something new at the player before boredom can even threaten to rear its head.

PREDATOR (1988)

Label: Activision, Mike Chilton

Predator is based on the classic 1987 film of the same name. Licenced games like this were frequently a disappointment for C64 owners. Companies loved to get a movie or television licence because they could slap the film poster on the box and entice gamers to part with their money with alluring cover art alone. A lot of the time though C64 users ended up with a shoddy game for their trouble. Games, for example, based on Big Trouble in Little China and Knight Rider are among the worst C64 games of all time. Caveat emptor was the best advice.

Predator was happily pretty good though and a game that has plenty of atmosphere. In the game you play Arnie's elite special forces character Dutch Schaefer and are dropped into a guerrilla festooned jungle. This isn't the only thing in the jungle though. There also happens to be a technologically advanced alien who is on Earth to hunt humans for sport. This game is a side scroller with pretty good graphics. Dutch and the jungle backdrops are both nicely conveyed. The early stages are more generic action fare but then the alien enters the fray - which you become aware of thanks to the screen depicting its laser sights and infra-red vision.

I find this game to be an admirable attempt to capture the spirit and plot of the Predator film and it has a very immersive aura. The flaws in the game are that it's quite short and can be frustratingly difficult. Nonetheless this game deserves a lot of credit for not just taking the licence money and running. They did actually put a lot of effort in here to give you a good game. There are some nice touches too here - like the way you can, as in the film, get Dutch covered in mud to make him less visible to the alien.

It is the level of detail in Predator that is impressive and shows that this wasn't just your bog standard licence grab. I like the way Arnie's character animates when you fire a gun. You really notice little things like this. Predator was a notoriously tricky game and many said they never finished it but if you are up for a challenge this will certainly test your resolve. I was sort of obsessed with this game for the atmosphere as much as anything. Maybe I was just relieved to finally play a movie tie-in that wasn't dreadful.

Predator is a game I have a lot of nostalgia for and - warts and all - this was a memorable experience on the C64 for me.

PROJECT FIRESTART (1989)

Label: Electronic Arts, Designer: Numerous

Project Firestart is a survival horror game - a very early entry in what would soon be a popular genre thanks to later games like Resident Evil. The player in this game is Jon Hawking - a government agent who has been sent to a research station Promentheus orbiting Titan, a moon of Saturn. The crew on the station have lost contact with Earth. Hawking must retrieve the scientific data on board the ship and then destroy it. The crew have been murdered and the ship has large creatures on it created by genetic engineering experiments on the ship. Hawking must find a way to kill one supercreature by finding a vulnerability using scientific methods.

SIA Agent Annar Kensan, who was working in secret with Dr.

Arno, survived by placing himself in cryosleep; upon Hawking's arrival on the Prometheus, he awakens. Also in cryosleep is Mary, another Firestart scientist who survived the massacre because she was placed in suspended animation after suffering a minor injury. The ending of the game varies depending on different actions taken by the player. This is obviously something that adds more depth to the gameplay and the chances of one returning to this game.

This is a very ambitious and interesting game for the era and something somewhat new at the time. The combat in the game is not the best but it has plenty of atmosphere to mitigate some of the flaws. This game was very well received upon its release and garnered 91% in ZZAP!64. Project Firestart is quite a bold game for the era and (unwittingly perhaps) anticipated the glut of survival horror games which would flood the markets in years to come. What is likeable about Project Firestart is that it takes the time to build up a backstory and world for the game to take place in but the actual game itself is more than worthy of that world and does full justice to the concept. This is a really good game for the time and worth exploring if you are partial to a bit of scary survival horror.

PROJECT STEALTH FIGHTER (1987) & GUNSHIP (1986)

Label: MicroPose Software, Designer: Numerous

Project Stealth Fighter is a military flight simulation game. This might not look amazing to modern eyes but it was state of the art in 1986 and showed what the C64 was capable of when stretched to its limits.

In the game, the player take on the role of a fictional fighter pilot flying missions of varying difficulty over four geographic locations: Libya, the Persian Gulf, the North Cape, and Central Europe. Project Stealth Fighter is not only immersive but also

addictive and creates a genuine sense of threat and danger as
you race to complete the missions.

Flight simulation games are not everyone's cup of tea (I'm
generally not the biggest fan of flight sims myself) but this
game was a cut above your average flight simulation game
with its depth of gameplay, strategy, and state of the art
presentation. This is one of those games that those who got
into it played for months. It's definitely a more substantial and
weighty game to take on than your average C64 release! By the
way, this game came with a huge manual which it was best to
read because it contained some very useful tips about strategy.

Equally as good as Project Stealth Fighter is the 1986
MicroPose game Gunship. In this game the player controls a
AH-64 Apache helicopter and takes part in five missions which
occur in various places around the world. You are of course
armed to the teeth in this helicopter with various missiles and
rockets. The landscapes scroll smoothly in this game and the
feeling of flying the helicopter feels realistic and satisfying. As
with Project Stealth Fighter the presentation of this game and
level of detail and gameplay depth is very impressive.

If you were partial to a military flight sim on the C64 then
Project Stealth Fighter and Gunship meant you were very well
catered for. Trivia - Gunship was supposed to be a city based
game inspired by Blue Thunder and Airwolf but this concept
had to be shelved because the designers found it too complex
and problematic to put city landscapes in the game.

Another military flight sim style game worth checking out is
Ace of Aces - a US Gold game from 1986. This game takes
place during World War II and has you controlling an RAF
Mosquito (the 'wooden wonder') on bombing missions over
Germany. The thing that distinguishes Ace of Aces from other
games is that although ostensibly a flight sim (of sorts) the
focus is more on arcade action than 'dry' realistic simulation.
The raids and dog fights are fun and the game looks terrific. I
love the depiction of the clouds in this game and it's fun the
way the weather can change and so you suddenly find yourself

in a storm. Ace of Aces is an attractive and interesting game on the whole. The only flaw though is that there are a limited number of missions and once you've completed these your motivation to go back to the game might be lessened somewhat. Ace of Aces was definitely once of those games that was crying out for more missions and a longer campaign.

If you are bored by military flight sims you could always try something different - like Steel Thunder for example. Steel Thunder is a tank simulation released by accolade in 1988. The player can choose from the M60A3, M1A1, M3 and M48A5 tanks. For each mission three other crew members are chosen. The crew members the player chooses from have different characteristics and specialties. There is a driver, gunner and commander view - the assistant gunner is simulated and these can each be controlled by the player by switching controls. The player can also just give commands. There is a training operation before the missions. There is a career path which can be saved. There are nine ammunition types. There are missions in Cuba, Syria and West Germany, with eight missions in each country.

Steel Thunder is a detailed tank simulation for the C64. The graphics are quite detailed and the game is very atmospheric. The different missions and the career path with different ranks and experience also helps longevity in the game. There is strategy involved in planning picking the crew and undertaking the missions. This is a very good tank simulation given the C64's limitations. One thing that may have made it better would have been some more variety in the landscapes though. If you like military simulations you should enjoy this game. It deserved better reviews than it garnered at the time.

Another military simulation that offers something different from the usual flight sims is Silent Service - a 1986 game by Sid Meier for MicroProse. Silent Service is set in the Pacific Ocean during World War II. You control a U.S. Gato-class submarine in action against Japanese shipping. Silent service is a very polished and well designed game and there are lots of nice touches like the way you choose when to attack. The gameplay is immersive and atmospheric and - all in all - Silent service makes an interesting change from military sims which focus on aircraft. Another naval sim that is worth a look is the 1986 Epyx game destroyer. Destroyer puts the player in the role of captain of a Fletcher-class destroyer in the Pacific theatre during World War II. Destroyer is pretty good for what it is but you'd probably need a high tolerance for military simulations and plenty of time and patience to get the most out of it.

RACING DESTRUCTION SET (1985)

Label: Electronic Arts, Designer: Rick Koenig, Connie Goldman

Racing Destruction Set is an isometric racer that doesn't look like much at first glance but is actually a very addictive and ingenious game. The big novelty here is that you can create your own tracks to race on and there is also a split-screen two-player mode. This game got an excellent reception upon its release and earned 95% in ZZAP!64. You can change the nature of the terrain you race on, customise the cars, and choose from a variety of vehicles. The vehicles available are a Can-Am sports car, a Jeep, a Lunar Rover, a dirt bike, a baja bug, a pickup, a Sting Ray, a stock car, a street bike, and an indy/grand prix car.

There are two modes in the game - racing and destruction. In the first mode you obviously have laps and rules. In destruction mode carnage is the goal and you are given various booby traps to deploy. Racing Destruction Set is basically like a computer game version of Scalextric! This game is great fun and kept kids entertained for hours on the C64 when it was released.

If you like games like this another one to consider is Simon

Pick's 1991 game Indy Heat. Indy Heat is a top down racing game. There are 10 tracks. The player has compete in and win 12 races. The car can be customised with brakes, tyres, engine etc to improve performance. The player starts with 3 coins. If the player loses a coin can be used to continue. A two player option is available. There were quite a few of these overhead racers on the C64 and this is one of the best. Even if you don't like overhead racers that much (and I'm really not the biggest fan of them myself) Indy Heat is still fun and stands out from the pack.

The racing in Indy Heat is very playable and quite addictive. One fun aspect is shunting the other cars during the race. The range of animations such as the cars, exhaust fumes and the pits are very good. There is range of tracks to play.

This is a great conversion of a game that was released in the arcade and then ported to the Amiga and Atari ST with very nice graphics and animation for the C64. This game really comes to life in two player mode and is very entertaining if you have someone to play against.

If you like games like Indy Heat you should check out BMX Simulator - which was released by Codemasters in 1986. BMX Simulator is a BMX bicycle race simulator. The race is viewed from top down. There are seven BMX tracks with ramps and bumps. There are tow riders in the race. Two player mode is available. This is a very fun game which was a budget title on its release. It has appealing graphics graphics and sound effects. It is very playable and is a simple but well made game. There are several tracks and some nice touches such as the bike slowing down when going through water. The controls are very intuitive too and there are some nice animations.

Overhead racers are not really my cup of tea but Indy Heat and BMX Simulator are worth a look if you are a fan of these types of games yourself. Another game I should mention in passing is the 1992 Codemasters game Slicks - another top down racer. This game is very popular and arguably the best of the top down racing genre on the C64. The racing in Slicks is fun and the graphics are crisp and colourful.

RAID ON BUNGELING BAY (1984)

Label: Broderbund, Designer: Will Wright

Raid on Bungeling Bay is a shoot em up game. In this top down game, the player controls a helicopter on a planetoid controlled by the Bungeling Empire. The Empire plans to take over Earth. The player has to bomb factories on islands while fighting off missiles, jet fighters and a battleship. The helicopter base is on a battleship which must be defended. The factories develop technology and if they are allowed to develop their weapons the enemy will become too powerful.

This is a classic strategy/shoot em up which looks simple is very playable and atmospheric. The sound effects compliment the game. The game has smooth scrolling in all directions and helicopter controls. Will Wright developed the game. He created Sim City and this game was a forerunner of that classic game. Raid on Bungeling Bay has factories and technologies that develop similar to Sim City.

Though a very different type of game, Bungeling Bay led directly (more or less) into Sim City. The NES version was a big hit which allowed Wright to have time to develop Sim City. Incidentally, Sim City was created for the C64 first in 1985 as Micropolis. Unfortunately an incomplete version of it was released later on the C64 in 1989.

The most obvious novelty in Raid on Bungeling Bay is that you can fly anywhere you want. This isn't a 1942 style shooter when you simply flow up the screen or even a dual side scroller. Raid on Bungeling Bay allows you to go anywhere you want. While the graphics are not astounding it is really the gameplay which makes this such a memorable experience. Blasting city targets is very engrossing and the dog fights will have you twisting and turning in your seat and satisfy action fans. This is a great little game from the early years of the C64 and great fun to play. Raid on Bungeling Bay is an oldie but a goodie.

RAID OVER MOSCOW (1984)

Label: Access Software, Designer: Bruce Carver

Raid over Moscow is an action game. In the game the player plays an American space pilot who has to stop nuclear attacks on North America by the Soviet Union. In the world of the game the USA has no nuclear weapons.

In Level 1 SAC (Strategic Air Command-Headquarter) we see a map of Soviet Nuclear bases and the launching of missiles.

In the 2nd Level the player has to manoeuvre a fighter jet out of a hangar.

Level 3 (The Attack) sees a side on scrolling sequence where the player flies a jet flying through Soviet territory avoiding obstacles and enemies missiles.

In Level 4 the player pilots a plane at the bottom of the screen which must destroy missile silos at the top of the screen.

Level 5 is The Kremlin and sees the player attack Moscow's government headquarters. The player controls the pilot at the bottom of the screen armed with a mortar. The Kremlin is at the top along with various snipers and tanks.

Level 6 is the Reactor where the pilot is at the bottom of the screen. He throws discs at a robot defending the reactor. Disks are limited and must be caught if they bounce back off the wall. The robot is destroyed by a disc bouncing off the wall and hitting the robot in the back.

Raid over Moscow was made by Beach Head's Bruce Carver and if you liked the two Beach Head games then you should enjoy this too. In many ways this game feels like another Beach Head entry but under another name. The graphics and sound effects in particular are very reminiscent of Beach Head II. It's nice by the way to have a genuine Cold War game on this list. Raid over Moscow might be a trifle tasteless but there's no doubt that the Soviets made great villains! This game is very atmospheric and very of its time. It is very enjoyable with the different elements. The graphics are fine and the animations are wonderful.

Trivia - a left-wing magazine in Finland protested against this game because they deemed it anti-Soviet. A member of the Finnish parliament also wanted the game banned. The game wasn't banned though and all the controversy made Raid over Moscow the biggest C64 seller of the year in Finland!

RESCUE ON FRACTULUS (1985)

Label: Lucasfilm Games, Designer: David Fox

Rescue on Fractalus is a first person sci-fi flight sim shooter. In the game the player is (as the title suggests!) on a rescue mission. Pilots have crash landed on a barren planet called Tepidi Vad Nerolei Rachcri. J'Haggari Kachatki aliens – known as Jaggies - are after them. The player pilots a Valkyrie fighter and has to rescue the pilots and shoot the enemies. A direction finder is used to locate the pilots. When a certain number of pilots have been rescued the level is complete and the player flies back to the base in orbit. The levels get harder, including night-time missions and kamikaze flying saucer attacks to contend with. There are sixteen levels.

Rescue on Fractalus has good graphics (the scrolling 3D landscapes were pretty state of the art for the time) and a great atmosphere with lots of nice touches. The gameplay is good with the game becoming increasingly difficult as the mission goes on. There are lots of atmospheric sound effects such as air locks opening which add to the game. Sometimes the alien "Jaggies" tap on the windscreen of the craft - which some people complained about as they thought it was too scary for their children!

Rescue on Fractalus was one if the first games for George Lucas's Lucasfilm Games. The game was intended to be a Star Wars related game but George Lucas decided not to do this in the end. Shooting the aliens was not a part of the game originally but George Lucas suggested it and it was put in the game. Rescue on Fractalus is a very interesting game and very ambitious for the era. One could argue that the tech in 1985 was not quite ready for a game this ambitious but it's a laudable effort nonetheless to stretch what the C64 might be capable of nonetheless.

The Lucasfilm games, as one might expect, were always very cinematic in their outlook and trying to give you the biggest and boldest experience they could within the confines of the C64 (and other systems). This level of ambition was very admirable and led to some fascinating games.

If you liked Rescue on Fractalus you should also play the 1986 Lucasfilm game Koronis Rift. Koronis Rift has a similar concept and gameplay and is arguably a more polished game.

In the game the player controls a surface rover vehicle to enter several "rifts" on an alien planet made up of fractal mazes. A lost civilisation known as the Ancients has left remarkable machinery, so-called "hulks", within these rifts which are guarded by various flying saucers.

Koronis Rift has the usual cinematic feel of the Lucasfilm games and some interesting puzzles to solve. It's a nice mixture of action and strategy. The game was designed for the Atari and then a special C64 version was made. The game was tweaked for each platform to take advantage of the strengths (and mitigate the weaknesses) of the Atari and C64 respectively.

Koronis Rift is most impressive in the way that the mountain backdrops put you in the heart of the action (and atmosphere) of the game. One must develop a knowledge of these surroundings if you are to be successful in the game.

ROCKETBALL (1985) & SPEEDBALL 2 (1991)

Label: IJK Software, Designer: John S. Sinclair

Rocketball is a sports simulation. In 2010 AD world disputes are now settled in the Rocketball arena with a violent sports game. Rocketball is played on a banked circular track - like a velodrome track. Points are scored by throwing a metal ball in a target. The players skate around the arena and can use elbows, knees and fists to take out opposing players.

There are four teams to choose from Houston (wearing blue), Tokyo (yellow), Moscow (burgundy) and Madrid (Green). The two teams have five players. There are five difficulty levels plus a two player mode. Games are ten minutes. The game is side scrolling from right to left.

Rocketball is a fun futuristic sports simulation based on the sport played in the 1975 science fiction film Rollerball. I'm not sure why this was not called Rollerball - maybe they could not get the licence or it was too expensive to do so? They basically just ripped-off the Rollerball concept for an original game in the end. Rocketball is very playable and the violent sport is fun to play. The ball is rolled along the floor of the arena and it must be picked up and then thrown into a hole in the wall. There is a fighting element to the game also as you can bash opponents to the floor to get the ball.

There are are what you might describe as serviceable graphics (the players are rather chuncky and the crowd backdrops don't have much detail or variety) in Rocketball but some nice animations and the game scrolls smoothly. The controls are fine although it is a bit fiddly sometimes to crouch and pick up the ball. As usual with these sports games there is a nice two player option. Rocketball is good fun on the whole and was something a bit different for C64 owners who were a trifle bored by endless soccer games or multi-sports simulations.

If you like Rocketball you should probably also check out the image Works game Speedball 2 by Carl Muller. Speedball is a futuristic cyberpunk sport in which teams of nine players play with a metal ball by hand. Points are scored by hitting targets in the playing arena, scoring goals, and injuring players from the opposing team. There are different modes: cup, league, knockout and practice. There is a multiplayer option. Games last 180 seconds. The view in the game is top down.

This is a great game based on ice hockey and handball. It is quite similar to the violent sport Rollerball as depicted in the 1975 science fiction film. The game Rocketball, as we just noted, did a similar thing.

The C64 Speedball 2 is a version of the game that was first produced for the Atari St and Amiga. Naturally the C64 graphics are not as good as those 16-bit versions but the gameplay is still very good with a fast paced game. The game has great colours which suit the futuristic setting, nice sound effects and a good music score. The game is a sequel to Speedball released in 1988. Both of these games are worth playing.

If you want a fast-paced sports simulation that it is a little bit different then both this game and Rocketball are a lot of fun.

ROCKET RANGER (1988) & SINBAD AND THE THRONE OF THE FALCON (1988)

Label: Cinemaware, Designers: Kellyn Beck (Rocket Ranger), Michael A. Knox (Sinbad)

Rocket Ranger is an action/adventure game. Set during World War II, the player is a US army scientist with a flying jet rocket pack who is battling against the Nazis. Futuristic artifacts are sent to the scientists from the future in which Nazi Germany won World War II. The Nazis are using a chemical called lunarium, a chemical found on the Moon. They drop it by Zeppelins on Allied nations and the chemical lowers the IQ of human males. The player must fly around the world stopping the Nazis from gaining the technology. This includes air fights, bareknuckle fights and attacking depots. The player must collect 5 parts for a rocket ship and 500 units of lunarium to fly to the Moon and close down the Nazi mines. A subplot involves talking to Dr Barnstoff and his daughter Jane (the love interest of the "film").

Another game element in Rocket Ranger is controlling five agents who must be placed on a world map to find hidden Nazi bases and create resistance movements to stop the Nazis progress towards the American heartland.

Rocket Ranger is a very pleasant cinematic experience from Cinemaware - in the style or the 30s/40s serials. The Rocketeer comics (which were turned into a sadly underrated 1990 film) seem to have been an obvious inspiration for this game. Rocket Ranger, originally made for the Amiga, pushes the C64 graphics and capabilities to the limit with great graphics and sound. The film has a great plot along with many wonderful humorous moments. The mini-games are varied and all the elements of the game are great to play. This is a terrific game if you like arcade adventures with a cinematic twist.

Another excellent Cineware adventure game is Sinbad and the Throne of the Falcon. The Caliph of Damaron wants to hand the regency if his Kingdom to his son Harum but to a spell has turned the Caliph into a falcon. Princess Sylphani has called upon Sinbad to break the spell. The player is Sinbad and must rescue the Caliph and protect the Prince and Princess. Sinbad uses his ship Sabaralus to search the area to find solutions. Four magical items must be found to return the Caliph to human form. In the game there are dialogues, strategy elements placing armies on a map, and action sequences. The action sequences are Sword fighting, fighting with a Cyclops using a slingshot, steering the ship through rocks and rescuing sailors, taking jewels from a statues eyes, shooting Pteranoxos creature and a platfprm sequence underground.

Sinbad and the Throne of the Falcon is another Cinenmaware product with great graphics and presentation and a number of games rolled into one. The storyline is very charming and it provides the usual cinematic experience the Cinemaware games aim for. The mini-games are nicely varied and the game is a fun experience. If you like theses sorts of games then Sinbad and the Throne of the Falcon is a polished and enjoyable experience.

SENTINEL (1984)

Label: Synapse Software, Designer: Bryan Brandenburg

Sentinel (not to be confused with a famous C64 game called The Sentinel) is a space 3D shoot em up game. The player has to defend a planet as Robert Reptile - a Jaralobian. The player has to select a difficulty level - from 5. There is a grid of the star system made up of 60 squares. Enemy and allied icons are in each grid. The player chooses an enemy in a grid section. The view is a 3D screen of the action with two guns at the bottom of the screen. The guns are fired via cursor.

Then the ship travels via warp speed to the sector where the enemy - such as an enemy space station or squadron - is engaged. During warp speed there are asteroids to contend with. There is a shield and energy meter and if these are low the player must go to a home base for repair. At the end of the game a rating is given based on the performance in the battle.

This is a very simple looking game but it has great 3D effects and sound. The game is very atmospheric. It is good fun with Star Wars style space fights and extremely addictive. It is very similar to the 1979 Atari game Star Raiders. There range of difficulty levels helps to sustain the playability of the game.

Sentinel is an interesting early C64 game because it gives the impression of 3D. I've always loved the presentation of this game too with the grids and hyper speed effects. It all has something of the atmosphere of computer graphics and designs in films of the era like The Last Starfighter and Star Wars. There is just something very appealing about the presentation in this game. The graphics are not amazingly elaborate but they are inventive. This game is a lot of fun to play. The re playability of this game is debatable but you should have a blast while you do play it. If you amp up the difficulty you can give yourself more of a challenge. The 2001 theme on the title screen is great too. This game actually got a budget re-release in Britain so was fantastic value if you came about it that way.

THE SENTINEL (1986)

Label: Firebird, Designer: Geoff Crammond

The Sentinel is a puzzle game that was something of a sensation when it arrived on the C64. The best way to describe this game would be to liken it to chess. The game takes place over a stunning 3D landscape of hills and valleys (the trees in this game always looked like Christmas trees to me!) and the aim of the game is to take take control of a number of checkerboard squares and climb higher - eventually dislodging the Sentinel who sits high above. You move the cursor at the square you want to occupy and must gradually absorb the energy of the Sentinel.

That synopsis barely scratches the surface of this intricate and intelligent game. This is a masterful piece of design and was quite unlike anything people had seen on the C64 at the time. I suspect a fair few younger C64 owners were rather bewildered by this game in 1986. If you've come here to waggle your joystick and shoot aliens then you've come to the wrong place with The Sentinel. The Sentinel is most definitely not that sort of game. It goes without saying that this won't be everyone's cup of tea but it would be ridiculous not to include a game this original and clever in any list of the best C64 games.

Though it might seem a little overwhelming at first, The Sentinel is not as complex as it might sound once you've mastered the basic functions and got a grasp of what you are actually supposed to be doing. This is a slow game but very immersive and because it is so vast in scope there is plenty of playability. If you do beat the game it goes back to the start. Geoff Crammond, the designer, said it never occurred to him that anyone might ever beat the game - thus explaining the lack of a distinct ending!

Although this is a slow and sedate sort of game the tension becomes unbearable at times and the ominous atmosphere is dread is generated right from the start by the spooky loading screen. If you take the time to learn how to play this game then many absorbing hours await. The most remarkable thing about this game (besides the genius concept and gameplay) is how Crammond was able to put a 3D landscape like this in the limited confines of the C64. The Sentinel is a genius piece of design but - happily - the game itself is also worthy of all the superlatives you can think of. By the way a sequel for this game titled Sentinel Returns was released on the Playstation and MS-DOS in 1998. This sequel earned some fairly decent reviews. The Sentinel is probably something of an acquired taste but it is a very rewarding and gripping experience if you fall for the highly immersive aura of the game.

SID MEIER'S PIRATES! (1987)

Label: MicroProse Software, Designer: Sid Meier

Sid Meier's Pirates! is a strategy/adventure game. In it the player plays a privateer (private individuals commissioned by governments to carry out quasi-military activities). The player can choose to hold allegiance to the Dutch Republic, Kingdom of England, Spanish empire or French Colonial Empire in the Caribbean. The player can change loyalties, hold multiple loyalties or turn to piracy. The player can attack enemy towns or ships, seek treasure, rescue family members, hunt pirates or trade to make money. The game ends when the player retires. A position is given from beggar to King's Advisor based on success in the game. Different eras can be chosen to start the game. 1600, 1620, 1640, 1660. The game is set in the Caribbean.

A classic game from Sid Meier (who was responsible for Civilization and F-15 Strike Eagle amongst numerous other classics), Meier said this game provided a chance to bring the film fantasy depiction of piracy to the computer game world. Pirates has many fun elements such as strategy, making money and swordfights. It is an open world game giving the player a variety in playing the game. The game has dynamic playing files meaning the game is randomised at the start. This means that every game is different. The relations between the countries and the economies of the cities are different. Also the player's choice of era and approach to the game makes for a different game each time.

Sid Meier's Pirates! has obviously dated somewhat since its release but it still looks pretty good and there's plenty of fun to be had here with sword fights and treasure hunts. If you have the patience to get into this game you will find it a rewarding experience with plenty of gameplay depth, a huge strategy component, and a great pirate atmosphere with plenty of timbers to be shivered. Some believe this is the greatest game ever made for the C64 and while that's purely a matter of personal taste (ZZAP!64 seemed to give this a very sniffy review and didn't really seem to get the game at all) there's no doubt that this is an ambitious and fascinating C64 game that is well worth playing if the like the sound of it but have never got around to playing it. Pirates is a fun adventure came which influenced many other classic open world games.

SKATE OR DIE! (1987)

Label: Electronic Arts, Designer: David Bunch, Stephen H. Landrum

Skate or Die! is a skateboarding sports simulation game. The player competes in five events. Freestyle ramp, ramp high jump, downhill race in a park, downhill race in a street and a pool joust. There are various characters in the game who are opponents in some events. For example, Rodney Recloose is a man with a purple mohican (who is based on the comedian Rodney Dangerfield) and his green haired son Bionic Lester. Up to eight players can compete.

Skate or Die is a very good multi-event sports game. The graphics are colourful and suit the style of the game. The animations are very smooth. There are humorous touches such as the "Rodney Dangerfield" character. Rob Hubbard provides a memorable soundtrack. The events are very playable and varied which is important in a multi-event game.

The game is similar to Epyx's games series - such as World

Games and Winter Games. Electronic Arts founder Trip Hawkins wanted to create a multi-event sports game as he saw that the Epyx series was popular. Some Epyx programmers such as Stephen Landrum and Michael Kosaka had left Epyx so they were hired to work on this game. This obviously means Skate or Die! has - enjoyably - an Epyx sportsgames type feel. An equally enjoyable winter themed sequel called Ski or Die was released in 1990.

Though a sports game entirely based around skateboarding might sound constrictive on the face of it the game has enough variety to overcome this potential pitfall. The events like the high jump (where you basically just to have to skate as high as you can off the top of the ramp) are fun but then you get the welcome addition of some street races. This variety stops the game from ever feeling too samey and gives you more stuff to play. It's always fun when a new event starts in this game and you are suddenly playing something different to the last time.

Skate or Die! is a classic game on the whole with lots of charm and great graphics.

If you are on the look out for another skateboarding game then you might like 720° - which was released by US Gold in 1987. This game is based on a Japanese arcade machine. In this game you are a skateboarder roaming around a neighbourhood and doing various stunts and tricks. This is a pretty decent game on the whole and all quite addictive and playable.

Another skateboarding game is SkateRock - which was released by Bubble Bus in 1987. In this you have to complete a course that is essentially a normal city street sort of scene. The graphics in SkateRock are pretty terrible but the gameplay isn't bad at all.

SOCCER BOSS (1986)

Label: Peasksoft/Alternative Software, Designer: Harry Whitehhouse

Have you ever wanted to try your hand at being the manager of a football team? Well, here's your chance. This is a football management game and was released in 1986 by Alternative software. The game had previously been released by Peaksoft in 1984 and was known as The Boss. In the game you take charge of an English football league team. There are four divisions and you start off in the fourth division. The aim is to get promoted to the first division. The player manages a squad of 15 players. The players have a rating out of 10 which goes up and down. Players can be bought and sold, their price depending on their rating. The formation can be chosen, with defence-midfield-attack given a rating out of 10. This allows the player to match up against the next opponents - the next opponent's rating is shown.

For the match, a basic green football pitch is shown and a noise is made after each minute goes past. When a goal is scored the screen flashes. After each match, the league table is shown and a news ticker shows injuries, transfers and other items such as ticket sales and other financial matters. All the headaches and ups and downs of being a football manager will be thrown your way in this game. It's up to you to make a success of it though. Will you be a success or a flop?

On the face of it this should be a dull text based repetitive game but it is really addictive. Although there are not many players in the game and they can play in any position, I always find myself wanting a certain player as he always scored the goals. Also the matches are quite tense - the screen flashes when a goal is scored but it waits 5 seconds to show who has scored. This is a game I still play today and it is fun to have on in the background on an emulator on windowed mode while doing something else.

This is the sort of game that will not be for everyone but I feel like this book has to have at least one football manager game and for some reason Soccer Boss is the game in this genre I always had a soft spot for. There were quite a few of these types of games on the C64 (including ones that allowed you to be a manager in other sports) and of the others Football Manager and Football Manager 2 are both well worth playing if you like Soccer Boss.

SPACE ROGUE (1989)

Label: Origin Systems, Designer: Paul Neurath

Space Rogue is a space flight simulator rather in the vein of Elite but with more advanced and colourful graphics. The company behind this went on to make the famous game Wing Commander so Space Rogue is sort of like a blueprint for Wing Commander. These space sims are not everyone's cup of tea (some people complain that they just end up getting hopelessly lost in space!) but if you do have a soft spot for these types of games the you should enjoy Space Rogue a lot.

The player in Space Rogue takes on the role of a character left stranded in a ship called the Jolly Roger after an attack by aliens named the Manchis. The game leaves it up to you to decide what you want to do from here on in. You have a range of choices. You can become a pirate, a merchant, and so on. You can visit space stations and dock. When you are in space you have the traditional first person cockpit point of view but there is a top down design for the space station interiors. The range of different styles stop the game feeling too samey.

This game feels much more advanced than Elite's vector graphics. The designs in Space Rogue are impressively colourful and detailed - not to mention solid. If you approach a space station you see it getting bigger and bigger. There are some nice little touches in the game like the way that an arcade game within the game can be played by the player's character. If one had a criticism of Space Rogue it would be that the frame rates are sometimes a little slow - especially when you are approaching a space station and the station is steadily increasing in size to denote your ever encroaching proximity. I suppose this is just an unavoidable consequence of the fact that Space Rogue is pushing the C64 to its limits - which is no bad thing as it illustrates the ambition of the game. Space Rogue is a terrific game on the whole. Part action game, part flight sim, part RPG, part adventure. If Elite didn't quite float your boat then you might like this more.

SPY HUNTER (1983)

Label: Bally Midway/Sega, Designer: George Gomez

In Spy Hunter the player is a secret agent driving a car equipped with multiple gadgets. The car turns into a boat when going over water during some levels. There are numerous enemies to be battled during the journey in cars, boats and helicopters. They are Road Lord (bullet-proof), Switch Blade - saws, The Enforcer - fires with a shot gun, Barrel Dumper - dumps a barrel in front of the player when in a boat, The Copter - drops bombs, Doctor Torpedo - fires torpedoes at the player's boat. A counter ticks down from 999 when the game first starts. In this time the player has unlimited cars. Once this ends the player only has one extra life. Cars are awarded for a certain number of points. Points are earned by killing the enemies.

The game is a port of the popular arcade game of the same name which was also released in 1983. It is based on the old classic James Bond series and you have a car laden with Bond style gadgets such as oil slicks, smoke screens and missiles. The original arcade game designer George Gomez was inspired to design the game after listening to a Bond film music compilation. He wanted to have the Bond theme for the music but could not get the licence. Instead they used the famous Spy Hunter theme - which is the theme to the Peter Gunn television series. The C64 Spy Hunter is a great version of the arcade game. The game has atmospheric graphics and smooth scrolling making it very addictive to play.

While the top down graphics of Spy Hunter seem fairly primitive today and the scrolling and action is well up to par and this justifiably ranks as one of the early classics of the C64. If you had a C64 in the early to mid eighties then you can almost guarantee that you played Spy Hunter at some point as it was one of those famous games that everyone seemed to have. Many eighties kids will have fond memories of hours spent playing this fun game.

By the way, what of genuine licenced James Bond games on the C64? Are any of these much cop? Sadly, official Bond games on the C64 were a mixed bag to say the least. By far the most atrocious is the 1985 Domark game A View To A Kill. This game must rank as one of my most disappointing gaming experiences on the C64. A game based on a Bond film! This must be good right? Wrong! A View To A Kill has three different sections which are essentially like mini-games. The first has you driving through Paris as Bond chasing May Day. Sounds great right? Unfortunately this must be the worst driving section of any game I have ever played. It's slow, graphically awful, and Paris consists of a series of brick walls. Next is City Hall where you must escape as the building is on fire. You have to get various locked doors open. This second section is as boring a the first. In the third section of the game you run around Zorin's mines - basically rubbish platform action! A View To A Kill is absolutely abysmal.

Somewhat better but still no classic was the game based on The Living Daylights a few years later. The Daylights C64 game is a side scrolling third-person shooter in the style of famous games of the era like Green Beret. Don't get too excited because Green Beret (though annoyingly tough) is vastly superior. In the Daylights game you wander across the screen from left to right and move a cursor around to shoot people who appear not only in front of you but also to the side at the top of the screen. This is the sort of mechanic that games like Operation Wolf would later use (only without the side scrolling).

The main problem in the Daylights game is that the mix of this cursor shooting mechanic with side scrolling is awkward. This mashing of different mechanics (including using the cursor to choose which direction to go) sounds quite ambitious for the time but the execution is fiddly. No other C64 game tried to copy the eccentric convoluted mechanics of the Daylights game and that tells you all you need to know about how successful it was. This game is also difficult at times. Reading around about the Daylights game I noticed a surprisingly large number of people say that they never got past the first level.

Side-scrolling games were all the rage back then because although there were 3-D games the technology to make 3-D games smooth, detailed, and fast was still something that largely needed to be invented. The breakthrough for 3D games came with Wolfenstein and then there was a giant quantum leap with Doom in the early 1990s. Doom was Wolfenstein times a million. Nineties games like Doom and Quake are the touchstones and trailblazers of the first-person shooter genre which still dominates gaming today.

As a white shirted pixel Timothy Dalton in the Daylights C64 game, you fight your way through eight levels (Gibraltar, The Lenin People's Music Conservatory, The Pipeline, The Mansion House, The Fairground, Tangiers, The Military Complex, Whitaker's House) to complete your mission. Bond can run, duck, jump and use weapons created by Q (including the Ghetto Blaster) and also take out enemies with his trusted Walther PPK. Although the controls are on the fiddly side, the Daylights game is not a completely terrible experience and far from the worst licenced game of this era. This game is at least reasonably playable.

One of the main stumbling blocks with Domark's A View To A Kill Game was that it was really three completely different mini-games in one package and none of these sections were satisfactory in isolation (in fact, the first part in particular where you are supposed to be driving around Paris, was absolutely terrible). The Living Daylights game is at least breezy and fast moving in comparison to A View To A Kill and has a more consistent concept and sense of purpose. The Living Daylights wants to keep things as simple as possible and be an arcade game where you are constantly shooting things all the way through. The gameplay never really changes. One nice thing about these old games is that you have unlimited ammo and never need to reload. When you play a game now you have to reload every ten seconds.

Domark's A View To A Kill game tried to be a driving game, a puzzle game, and (finally) a platform game but none of these individual sections were any good and the game felt like it was all over the place. All the individual levels in A View To A Kill felt half-arsed. The main criticism of the Daylights game was that it was merely a Missile Command clone (in that you follow a cursor to shoot targets which appear) dressed up in different graphics. The Daylights gameplay becomes samey after a while but at least some effort is made to make the various backdrops look different. It's a shame though that the game doesn't include Kara and there is no car section either.

As ever with C64 games, the James Bond theme is murderously mangled by the audio technology of the time. Bond is supplied with various different weapons in the game by Q. These include a bazooka and crossbow. While the playability and durability of the Daylights game is questionable, at least you can say that a modicum of effort went into it. The Living Daylights game doesn't feel like a completely lazy licenced cash grab but isn't anything to write home about either. It's nice though to have a Timothy Dalton Bond video game, however primitive it might seem today in a world of games like Doom Eternal.

In 1988, Domark bravely ventured back into the world of Bond games with Live and Let Die. A game based on Live and Let Die sounds sounds great right? Well, don't get your hopes up too much. For one thing this game didn't even begin life as a Bond game. It was supposed to be a boat chase game called Aquablasters and a follow-up to Buggy Boy. Domark simply bought the game and slapped Live and Let Die on top of it. I suppose they figured that as the film Live and Let Die has a lengthy boat chase sequence, Aquablasters, with a few modifications, would make a good adaptation.

Domark's Live and Let Die is very forgettable on the whole. It's just a bog standard racing game only on water rather than a road. This is the sort of thing you would have bought if it was a budget title and then played for a few hours and completely forgot about. The most disappointing thing about the game is that it only consists of boat racing and makes no attempt to incorporate other aspects of the film. Live and Let Die is not the worst game ever made but it is very average and a fairly lazy sort of licenced game. By the way, the rendition of the 007 theme in this game is absolutely dreadful.

The best of the C64 Bond games arrived in 1989 with Domark's Licence To Kill. This game was released on both the Commodore 64 and the Amiga. The game is a top down vertical scrolling action shoot em up where you pursue villain Franz Sanchez through various levels. The game starts in the vein of other top down shooters like 1942. You control a helicopter and battle your way through Florida landscapes blasting anything in sight. The gameplay in the first level is sort of like Space Invaders except you can move the helicopter forward and back and have to shoot numerous ground targets in addition to other aircraft. It's nothing radical or amazing but competent enough as an undemanding shooting level to begin the game.

The second level of the Licence To Kill game has Bond on foot shooting it out the army of Sanchez. The game becomes more of a Commando/Who Dares Wins II clone at this point although nowhere not as much fun as those two games. It does though at least freshen the game up and stop the gameplay from becoming too repetitive. You do get another helicopter section after this but this one is different because you are being dangled below the helicopter as Bond (as in the PTS of the film). It's to the credit of the game that they have these different sections but that they all feel part of one overall game rather than completely disjointed (as in the case of Domark's awful A View To A Kill game).

You also get a plane escape level and a water chase level - which are both good. The last section of the Licence To Kill game is the tanker chase. This section is basically Spy Hunter. You just race up the screen in a tanker and try and force other trucks off the road. The game is nothing special on the graphics front (though pleasantly colourful) and the over familiarity of this type of game (of which there were billions on the C64) makes the gameplay get old quite fast in certain levels. Mixing up the gameplay with slightly different sorts of sections was therefore very welcome.

The lack of originality in the Licence To Kill game is at least compensated for by the variety. The different sections do feel different (a contrast to the Daylights C64 game where although the backdrops changed the gameplay stayed exactly the same) and it's fun that they've tried to include the big action setpieces from the film. The makers of the Licence To Kill game were allowed to read some of the script in preparation for their game and they do a reasonable job of capturing the main action scenes of the movie within the constrictive confines of the C64. The programmers of the game even visited Pinewood Studios and met Cubby Broccoli. Licence to Kill's game earned a respectable 80% in ZZAP!64 (the most famous British gaming magazine of the era) and was better received than The Living Daylights game.

Licence To Kill is probably not what you would call an unqualified classic but my nostalgia goggles have a soft spot for this game simply because the previous few Bond games

had been so disappointing. Licence To Kill was - happily -
much better and (at long last!) gave C64 owners a pretty
decent Bond game. More than anything it is the game's
determination to be faithful to the film that gave it bags of
charm and likeability for me.

SPY VS SPY (1984)

Label: First Star Software, Designer: Nick Scarim

Spy vs Spy is a strategy game. In the game the player plays a
spy who is trying to kill another spy using weapons and traps.
One spy is dressed in white, the other in black. The game is
split screen with each spy having their own scrolling section.
The spies are in an embassy. The player has to collect items in
a briefcase - passport, money, key and secret plans, and exit
the building before the other or before their time runs out.
After a player dies they come back to life but 30 seconds is
taken off their timer. A limited number or traps can be used by
each spy. Solutions to the traps can be found. The spies can
also engage in hand to hand combat. The game can be played
by two players. For one player there are different difficulty
levels which changes the number of rooms, number of traps
and time available. The computer I.Q. can be changed.

Spy vs Spy is an extremely fun strategy game. The split screen
element is perfect for the game as the two spies battle it out
using booby traps and even fighting. There are lots of
humorous touches with the characters reactions to the
onscreen action. A memorable tune accompanies the action.
The nature of this game lends itself to the two player option.

The game is based on Mad Magazines Spy vs Spy cartoon.
There were two sequels: Spy vs Spy II The Island Caper in
1985, Spy vs Spy III Arctic Antics - both (especially the second
one) are as well regarded as the original. If you like games that
require some strategy and cunning and also ones that are

rather tongue-in-cheek you should have some fun with this.

Spy vs Spy was a huge seller on the C64 and its mix of humour and strategy made it a fairly beloved game in no time at all. This is arguably one of the most famous C64 games and nearly everyone will have heard of it and possibly even played it too. You should definitely have a look at this game if you haven't encountered it before and the first sequel (which had a novel new setting and improved graphics) is a must play too if you like the first game. This game was ported to the Atari and various other systems with great success. The fun concept of the game was a hit on more than one platform.

STUNT CAR RACER (1989)

Label: MicroPose, Designer: Geoff Crammond

Stunt Car Racer is a racing game in which one drives around (and frequently up!) elevated tracks with no barriers. This gives the impression of being on a huge winding up and down rollercoaster. You have a turbo boost to make the car go faster but the turbo is limited and only be used so often. The single player game uses a league table system. The Amiga version had a two-player mode but, alas, that isn't an option here.

Stunt Car Racer looks rather primitive today to modern eyes but it was something of a miracle at the time. It was not thought possible to make a 3D racing game of this type on the C64 but Stunt Car Racer achieved the impossible and earned glowing reviews. The most important thing about the game is despite the fact that the curvy and elaborate tracks are probably taking up a lot of the programme space as they load the game doesn't sacrifice fluidity. The impression of speed in the game is most impressive and makes Stunt Car Racer an exhilarating experience at its best. This game would have been awful if it took place at a crawling speed but the forward motion of the car and scrolling track all give one the impression that you are moving at a high velocity.

There are eight tracks in Stunt Car Racer and each presents a different and dextrous challenge. The game supplies a number of computer controlled players to compete against. This is a really fun game as you leap over gaps in the track and frenziedly try to keep your car on the right path. While this game looks simple today it was an absolute state of the art design for the time for the impression of speed it generated and the solid vector style graphics. Many believe this was the best racing game created for the C64 and while it's obviously all done to personal taste it would be fair to say that Stunt Car Racer is a contender for that prestigious title.

One other incredible thing about Stunt Car Racer is that it has a physics engine which makes the game seem (in so far as a stunt car game can be realistic) very realistic. The damage you do to the car is meticulously logged and the impact of great jumps is felt by the player. This is a great game on the whole and all the more remarkable for the fact that it smashes through a technical glass ceiling and shows that the C64 was capable of even more than people suspected at the time. Stunt Car Racer was a genuine technical marvel for its time and a genius piece of game design. It might seem dated today but this was an amazing experience back in the late 1980s.

SUMMER GAMES II (1985)

Label: Epyx, Designer: Numerous

Summer Games II is a multi-event sport simulation. The eight sports are triple jump, rowing, javelin, equestrian, high jump, fencing, cycling and kayaking. Events can be played individually or you can just play all of them. Up to eight players can compete. Gold, silver and bronze are awarded for each event. Players can choose from a selection of nations to compete from. This is the second in Epyx's famous games series. This one features some wonderful animations and depictions of the various sports. The controls are very good, providing a challenge and not relying on Daley Thompson's Decathlon style joystick waggling - apart from the cycling to a degree.

There is a good range of sports in this entry too giving the game a nice Olympic feel. A nice touch is the opening and closing ceremonies. The ceremonies are an indication of how much care Epyx have taken with the presentation of the game. As soon you see this ceremony you know you are in safe hands and set for a great game. There is a good musical accompaniment with different compositions for each event. The events are all pretty good. The javelin is a thing of beauty as you loft that spear into the air and the triple jump is fun too. In terms of graphics, the equestrian is probably least impressive as they obviously had to animate a horse - this being done to reasonable but not brilliant effect.

The fencing and cycling are fun because they involve some duels and the high jump is pretty good too. Although this is ostensibly an arcade game the athletics events are actually surprisingly realistic in this game. The kayaking at the end is top down and rather different to what has come before so adds some variety. One might argue that having two water events in the game was one too many but they are both different enough to justify their own existence. It's a shame I think that Epyx never included boxing in any of these games. It would have been fun to see Epyx have a bash at a little boxing simulation.

Summer Games II is a classic game that most C64 owners will have fond memories. The variety of sports on offer here means that the game has a lot of playability and is one you can return to again and again. This is truly one of the great C64 games. It goes without saying that if you love this game you should of course also play the original - which is equally as polished and playable and offers a range of events that include diving, the pole-vault, and gymnastics. The vintage Epyx sports games were always terrific fun and fully deserving of their lofty status as classics of the C64.

SUPER CYCLE (1986)

Label: Epyx, Designer: Stephen H. Landrum

Supercycle is a motorcycle racing game. The aim to is to get to the finish within a time limit on each level. Later levels include obstacles such as oil, ice and barriers. There are three levels. The player competes against two racers. After every three levels is a bonus round where the players earns points for driving over flags. This is a typically slick Epyx game for the C64. There are a variety of tracks: grass, desert, winter and even a very pleasant looking city track. There is some night time racing, as well as racing in a storm with thunder. This gives the game a great atmosphere.

One feature I always enjoyed in Super Cycle was that the bike colour and style and colours of the leather jacket of the rider could be chosen. It is a fun touch. Perhaps some music during racing would have been good - but there are some wonderful sound effects instead. The game has very good animation with a very well executed 3D track. Super Cycle is inspired by the Sega arcade game Hang-On. Though the graphics are not astounding (the bikes and riders are a trifle blocky) the backdrops make up for this.

More than anything what makes Super Cycle stand out from the pack is the sense of speed that is generated - something which is obviously very important in a racing game! When you play Super Cycle the road whizzes past and you feel like you are really going at a terrific clip. This sense of speed makes staying on the track and overtaking other riders not only more fun but also more challenging.

Super Cycle is a really solid racer on the whole. It has some nice touches - like the way you lean around corners like in a real race. The backdrops (puffy clouds!) break up the monotony and stop it from all feeling the same and the difficulty levels mean that this will be a decent challenge for even the most adept keyboard racer. Some music would have been nice and I'm not sure how often you would return to this once you had sampled all the tracks and beaten all the difficulty levels but there's no doubt at all that you'll have a blast when you play the game for the first time. Super Cycle is one of the best C64 racing games and great stuff.

10TH FRAME (1986)

Label: Access Software, Designer: Bruce and Roger Carver

10th Frame is ten pin bowling simulation. Up to eight players can compete in a league or open format. The player has two attempts to knock over 10 pins. The bowling lane is shown behind the player in a 3D perspective. The player can move and choose a bowling angle with a cursor before delivering the ball. To bowl, the fire button is pressed and when the required power is on the power meter, the fire button is unpressed. Another meter chooses hook/spin power and is then used and the fire button must be pressed when the bar is in the correct hook zone spot. There are three difficulty levels: kids, amateur and professional.

This was written by Bruce and Roger Carver - who produced the classic golf simulation Leader Board. The game is similar with the same graphics and controls. The smooth animations, sound effects and controls make it a pleasure to play - just like Leader Board. There is a multiplayer option and a league format too. Up to eight player can compete individually in open bowling or teams with up to four players and a team name can compete in a league. The only criticism one might venture is that 10 pin bowling is a sport that could be presented with more humour as a C64 game but the game still has a great relaxing atmosphere.

I've never actually been bowling myself but this game seems like a pretty accurate depiction of the real thing. If you've played Leader Board the control mechanics of the game are a doddle and very well designed and the visual presentation is excellent. 10th Frame is simply a very polished, playable, and enjoyable game with great graphics and animation. The learning curve is steep enough to make the game challenging and it is always satisfying when you mow down a good number of skittles with a well placed strike. The only complaint one might venture about this game is its replayability. Once you've played it a lot you might not have the motivation to go back to it too often but it is undoubtedly a very relaxing and pleasurable game to have a quick go on now and again.

THE TRAIN: ESCAPE FROM NORMANDY (1987)

Label: Accolade, Designer: J. Stuart Easterbrook, Lise Mendoza

The Train: Escape to Normandy is an action/simulation game. The player is Pierre LeFeu who has hijacked a steam train to escape Nazi Germany to save French paintings during World War II. The train has to be driven and Nazi planes fought off with anti-aircraft guns in the train. Gunboats have to sunk, bridges must be taken and cover must be given when the train stops at stations to be resupplied with coal and water. This is an atmospheric, cinematic World War II game from Accolade and the story is very good. The graphics are dark and wintry and really suit the tone and story of the game. There is variety in the game and it can be played differently each time it is played. The game is based on the 1964 film The Train.

The Train sort of plays like an updated version of Beach Head with better graphics and a different setting. The various sections in the game are all good fun and prevent it from becoming too samey (the rail shooter segment in the train station probably would have outstayed its welcome in the end if had constituted more of the game). What is great about this game is that it flirts with being a military simulation game but isn't actually one at all. It's more of an arcade game but presented with the polish and cinematics one would expect of a military simulation. What this essentially means is that you don't have to like military simulations to enjoy The Train. There's plenty of shooting and hands on action to keep you engaged.

By the way, driving the actual train in this game is a lot of fun and strangely engrossing. The graphics depicting all the levers and gauges are fantastic and you see little trees go past as you make progress. This is one of those games that got decent reviews when it came out but then became something of a cult classic as its reputation grew over time. The train driving aspects and the other strategy elements in The Train are not too long or dull and are broken up with the shooting action elements. One other interesting thing about the game too is that you have a certain freedom of movement when it comes to choosing where to go. This is a really good game on the whole and a nice middle ground between military simulation and arcade action.

TURRICAN (1990)

Label: Rainbow Arts, Designer: Manfred Trenz

Turrican is a side-scrolling action game which is similar to Metroid. You play a bio-engineered warrior who must liberate the man-made planet Alterra from a dastardly villain named MORGUL (an AI villain to boot). This is a brilliant and colourful shooter which breathed new life into the platform genre on the C64 with its fast paced action and detailed backdrops. You basically run and jump across various landscapes blasting everything in sight. The shooting aspect to the game is satisfying and fun and the platforming is pretty good too. Turrican was an example of how the tech of the C64 was perfectly capable of handling a side scroller every bit as frantic and fun as anything on the consoles.

Turrican is basically like having a machine from an eighties arcade on your television screen. While that doesn't like much today it was a very big deal in the C64 era. You could finally get the arcade experience at home with games like Turrican. The graphics are colourful and vibrant with many interesting landscapes to jump around and navigate. The weapon effects are also excellent - as is the sound. The controls are easy and responsive and the mix of blasting action and platform capers is highly entertaining. C64 owners must have lost days of their life to this game as it is very addictive and playable.

By the way, I could just have easily chosen the 1991 sequel Turrican II: The Final Fight for this book as the game is equally good (if not better - the reviews were even more glowing than the original) - which definitely should be played if you like Turrican. Both of these games really push the C64 to its limits and are fantastic examples of how great the C64 could be at its very best. If you like action games you should definitely have a look at the Turrican series. Turrican and Turrican II are amongst the most purely entertaining and fun games of the C64 era and both are very highly recommended.

ULTIMA IV: QUEST OF THE AVATAR (1986)

Label: Origin systems, Designer: Richard Garriott

Ultima IV - Quest of the Avatar is the fourth part of the Ultima series. The game has you trying to become the Avatar - the source of all wisdom. As one might expect there are many dungeons to be explored and monsters to battle. If you like RPGs then this was one of the best on the C64 and had quite a sophisticated concept in the game in that you are awarded for making the right moral choices. You can buy and sell in the game, cast spells, and a new feature has other characters fighting alongside the hero.

One of the nice things about this game is that it isn't linear. It's up to you what you do and in what order. Ultima IV - Quest of the Avatar was an immersive and addictive experience for anyone who falls under its (ahem) spell and it had plenty of gameplay depth and longevity to keep you going back and exploring more of the game. Graphically this game is nothing special (the layout is similar to Ultima III) but it does have plenty of atmosphere and the music is appropriately dark and dashing. There's a clever touch in this game in that you don't choose your character by traditional means. You have to attend a tarot reading at the start and this tarot reading ascribes your characteristics.

Another nice touch is that in the game you travel around and must win allies to join your team. The exploration aspect to the game is fun and Ultima IV will take weeks and months to beat. If you like RPGs and Dungeons & Dragons this you should have a lot of fun with Ultima IV - Quest of the Avatar. This game was a huge hit across many platforms and earned excellent reviews. The stature of this game seems to have grown over time and it is now even more highly regarded in vintage gaming circles. It goes without saying by the way that if you enjoy this you should also check out the other Ultima games.

URIDIUM (1986)

Label: Hewson Consultants, Designer: Andrew Braybrook

Uridium is a top down side scrolling shoot em up game. Enemy super dreadnoughts are in orbit. They are draining mineral resources from planets in the Solar System for use on their ships. The player controls a Manta Class Space fighter and must destroy each dreadnought. Enemy fighters must be destroyed. Surface ships are then destroyed. Land on the dreadnought to remove fuel rods, then take off as the dreadnought vaporizes. Fifteen dreadnoughts have to be destroyed.

This is a very impressive and stylish shoot em up from the creator of Paradroid – Andrew Braybrook The controls are very good and the player's ship is very responsive. The graphics and animations are good too with a metallic bass relief theme. The effect where the dreadnought dissolves as the players ship flies away is very good. There is a great use of the colours. The fast scrolling is very smooth and attractive. Braybrook wanted to recreate the fast smooth scrolling that was seen in arcade machines. He did this by maximizing the C64 refresh rate and cutting back on some other aspects of the game such as the screen size rows.

One nice touch is to fly the ship under parts of the super structure and to fly the ship on its side. The game is quite tough which adds to the longevity of the game. I have to be honest, I was always a bit rubbish at Uridium but it is one of the most polished and impressive shooters from the golden era of the C64. The constant changing of the colour backdrop stops the visual presentation from becoming too samey and the speed of the game remains impressive. Be warned though that Uridium is a very challenging game. If you are hopeless at these types of shooters it can be frustrating but practice makes perfect and if you ARE good at these types of games then you should relish the challenge posed by Uridium.

It's probably worth mentioning Andrew Braybrook's follow-up game Alleykat - which also came out in 1986. Because he had just made Paradroid and Uridium, Braybrook was sort of like the Steven Spielberg of the British games scene at the time and anything he did was highly anticipated. Alleykat had similar graphics to Uridium and was rather like a cross between a shoot em up and a racing game. Though quite well regarded it didn't set the world alight though (the gameplay was felt to be quite shallow and it was somewhat caught between two stools in that it wasn't quite a classic shoot em up nor a great racing game) and felt like a creative backward step after Paradroid and Uridium. You should take a look at Alleykat if you like Braybrook's other games but don't expect it to be quite up to the standards he set with his earlier games.

WASTELAND (1988)

Label: Electronic Arts, Designer: Alan Pavlish

Here's something a bit different. Wasteland is a post-apocalyptic role playing game. The game takes place in the aftermath of World war III. The use of atomic weapons has devastated the planet and left areas high in radioactive waste. The protanganists of the game are Desert Rangers - military style survivors who must explore this ravaged and ruined landscape to search for food, medicine, shelter, and safety. Naturally there are plenty of problems in a post-apocalyptic world of destruction. Everything from rabid dogs to other survivors must be survived if one is to make progress.

Wasteland was essentially used as the blueprint for the much later Fallout series. Although the 1980s was a time of high nuclear paranoia, post-apocalyptic games were still something of a novelty so Wasteland was an exciting experience for home gamers in 1988. Wasteland allows the player to build up the statistics and strengths of the characters through combat and acquiring items and weapons. If you get hold of a water bottle for example you won't suffer from heat stroke. The AI in the game is quite impressive and so the characters have what feel like their own little quirks and behave in a fairly realistic way. Wasteland has an interesting plot too in that the player must uncover a large secret which threatens to destroy what remains of humanity.

If you like these types of games and get into Wasteland then you've got hours of immersive fun in front of you because this game is not only well designed but also compelling and a very rewarding experience. More than anything it is the setting which makes this game so memorable. The unavoidably dark nature of the story immediately makes this game morbidly fascinating and gripping and is a change of pace from the usual Dungeons & Dragons style role playing games. A lot of people say that Wasteland was their favourite game on the C64. Because this game has such a legion of fans it has had remasters and special re-releases over the years. This is one of the most memorable games in the C64's later era and well worth the effort to track down. Wasteland is arguably the best RPG ever made for the C64 and will keep you going for weeks and months if you like these types of games.

THE WAY OF THE EXPLODING FIST (1985)

Label: Melbourne House, Designer: Gregg Barnett

The Way of the Exploding Fist is a justifiably famous karate fighting game. The player takes part in a series of one on one karate challenges. After a victory the player moves on to a more difficult opponent. The player has to get two ying yang icons to win the fight - half an icon is awarded for a good move, a whole one for a great move (this is the shobu nihon kumite scoring system). This is a classic C64 martial arts game. It is very playable with great animation in the combat and seventeen actions to choose from when fighting. There are a number of backgrounds which makes the game more varied.

One nice touch in Exploding Fist is the old karate expert watching on in the background. Another thing which makes the game is the great music. Neil Brennan based it on the 1952 orchestral piece Dance of the Yao People. There are great sound effects too and it makes a good 2 player game. Way of the Exploding Fist was very impressive for the era and the blend of superior graphics, enjoyable combat, and fun backdrops make it a pleasure to play. The sound effects are excellent too - with appropriately bone crunching sonic flourishes when you put an opponent down for the count! This was an amazing game for the time and along with International Karate took the fighting game on the C64 to a whole new level. The Way of the Exploding Fist is a genuine C64 classic.

There was a 1986 sequel to this game titled Fist 2: The Legend Continues. In the game an evil warlord has destroyed all the temples of the Exploding Fist. Ancient scrolls have been buried in the rubble. The player must retrieve the scrolls and defeat the warlord's fighters in the warlord's domain. The scrolls are found in various places such as caverns. Eight scrolls must be found. Finding a scroll gives more energy and another life. When fighting enemies in one on one karate fights the player has to wipe out the enemies energy bar.

Fist 2 seems to divide opinion as a game. The game tries to open up the world of Exploding Fist by having the character explore the surroundings (as opposed to just fighting someone in a static backdrop). Critics felt though that the game featured too much wandering around in caves and not enough fighting. One can see their point. Though the backdrops are nice it soon gets a bit dull wandering through caves and climbing down ladders when you just want to punch someone! Fist 2 is a very atmospheric game though and probably worth a look if you liked the first one.

What other fighting games on the C64 are worth a look when it comes to martial arts? Well, we've done International Karate, Fist, and The Last Ninja and the rest are a mixed bag. One game that is probably worth a look is Yie Ar Kung Fu - which was released by Imagine in 1985. This game was based on a 1984 Japanese arcade machine where you play a Bruce Lee type kung fu master who has to take on various opponents. Yie Ar Kung Fu seems more blocky and cartoonish than Exploding Fist but it is decent undemanding fun. One good thing about the game is that the fighting is pretty fast and furious - which is obviously good because there's nothing worse than a slow kung fu game. One nice thing about Yie Ar Kung Fu too is that it's a very colourful game and the backdrops change frequently. Yie Ar Kung Fu is not bad for what it is but it does feel rather lightweight in comparison to the top table of martial arts games where International Karate and Exploding Fist are seated.

Yie Ar Kung Fu got a sequel a year later which is generally regarded to be inferior to the original. The sequel is rather bonkers with crazy opponents and an even more cartoonish feel than the first game. You can walk around more in this game (shades of Fist 2) and the graphics seem like a downgrade on the original. What really negates
Yie Ar Kung Fu II is the difficulty spike and the fact that the control system seems askew. In fact, some even complained that you never quite felt in control of your character in the first game and it is even worse in the sequel. The first Yie Ar Kung Fu is worth a look but you should probably approach the sequel with caution - or at the very least lowered expectations.

An interesting if slightly disappointing kung fu game is Karateka - which was released in 1985. Karateka was designed by Jordan Mechner - who would later go on to create the legendary Prince of Persia. Karateka has the player as an unnamed hero who ascends a mountain into Akuma's fortress to rescue Princess Mariko. As you might expect, you fight various people along the way. Karateka is a beautiful looking game. The characters are detailed and wonderfully animated and the backdrops are pretty good too as you fight your way further into the fortress. Here's the problem though: the game is too slow! Because of its laggy pace the combat in Karateka is never satisfying and it feels like everything is happening in slow motion. It's a shame really because Karateka could potentially have been a classic game.

Perhaps the best fighting game outside of Exploding Fist and International Karate is the 1985 System 3 release Bangkok

Knights. This is essentially a kick boxing game and you'll fight opponents both in the street and the ring. This is a very impressive looking game as the characters are huge and nicely animated and everything is very colourful. The combat is pretty good fun too with great animations. The only problem with the game is that it isn't very difficult and this means that replayability might not be the most enduring. Still, Bangkok Knights is a really good game overall and one you should definitely take a look at if you like vintage beat em ups.

Another fighting game worth playing is the 1986 Martech release Uchi Mata (which was known as Brian Jacks Uchi Mata in Britain). This is a judo game and fairly realistic when it comes to moves and strategy. The graphics are a little blocky in Uchi Mata and nothing to write home about but the gameplay is challenging and very good. Another game worth a look is the 1987 Imagine release Renegade. This game is based on a Japanese arcade machine. It's a side-scrolling beat em up in which you play a New Yorker who has to rescue his girlfriend from street thugs by beating up an assortment of dubious characters in an urban setting. Renegade is pretty decent fun.

WINTER GAMES (1985)

Label: Epyx, Designer: Numerous

Winter Games is a winter sports competition game. Up to 8 players compete in the event, choosing which nation they want to represent. Players can compete in all events or only a selection. The sports are Hot Dog (freestyle skiing), Biathlon, Figure skating, ski jump, speed skating, free skating and bobsleigh. Winter Games is the third of Epyx's multi events sports games - after Summer Games I and II. The game has wonderful graphics for the time which are still good today - the graphics and snow festooned winter settings are rather charming. Pictures from the 1984 Winter Olympics in Sarajevo were used to create the wintry backdrops.

The sports in Winter Games are fun and varied. The controls can be a tad fiddly at first but they work and help the longevity of the game as they have to be mastered. Perhaps a skiing event could have replaced one of the figure skating events (although the slalom skiing did appear in 1986's World Games, another game in Epyx's sports series). The game was produced by Epyx and another company called Action Graphics as Epyx was busy making Summer Games II. Epyx wanted to get the game released for Christmas 1985 so they managed to overcome some technical problems and changed some of the game to make sure it was completed. For example, a sequence of the bobsleighers pushing the sled at the start was removed.

This is a really excellent game. I love the biathlon because it's almost a game unto itself as you explore an enjoyably snow glazed landscape. The figure skating is not my favourite event but beautifully animated. The ski-jump is very engrossing because you must control the flight of the jumper to achieve distance and secure a safe landing. The speed skating adds an enjoyable race element to the game and then you have the bobsleigh - which is probably the most fun of all. The bobsleigh ice course you race down has some great scrolling for the era and gives the player a good sense of speed and velocity. Winter Games is great fun on the whole. These Epyx sports simulations were a must for C64 owners and Winter Games happily continued the high standards set by previous entries.

A rather cheeky mimic of Winter Games titled Winter Olympiad was released by Tynesoft in 1988. The game has the usual winter events like biathlon, ski jump, etc, and is passable enough - earning 66% in ZZAP!64. It doesn't quite have the polish and class of the Epyx games though. If you are on the look out for another winter themed sports game you might want to consider playing the 1993 Thalamus game Winter Camp. Winter Camp is an arcade game. The player is Maximus Maus, a mouse ranger who works at the Nice 'n' Icy winter camp. The mouse undertake a series of challenges to save the camp from an avalanche.

The first challenge is a speed skating test. The second more skating with picking things on the way and avoiding obstacles. The third involves shooting snowballs. The fourth challenge involves patrolling a river. The fifth challenge is a music note memory game in a cavern. The sixth s skiing game. The seventh involves rolling downhill in a snowball. The eighth a mountain climb with a fight with a large bird at the top.

Winter Camp is a fun and eccentric game. There are eight stages - essentially mini-games - which are varied. The graphics are very colourful and fun. There are many amusing moments. It is very playable and a good game to play during the cold winter months. One small fault is the speed skating challenge at the start which involves waggling the joystick which was always mildly annoying due to the wear and tear on the joystick! It is a sequel to Summer Camp, which is a similar game to Winter Camp, but set in - as the title suggests - the summer.

WIZBALL (1987)

Label: Ocean, Designer: Chris Yates

Wizball is a shoot em up game. It is set in Wizworld where a villain called Zark has stolen all the colour. The player is controlling a green sphere - who along with his cat Nifta - must restore the colour of the world. There are eight levels. Each level starts off grey and the player has to collect red, blue and green colours to colour the levels. Bouncing spheres when shot release the colours. The player can access the first three levels at first - and move between them. Pearls can be collected to make the player's ball more dextrous. The cat as collects the paint and is controlled by the player by holding down the fire button and moving the joystick - the Wiz ball does not move during this time. A two player version is also available with separate player playing the Wiz and the cat. When all the levels are colourised the game starts again with harder enemies.

Wizball was a nice reminder that the shoot em up, a genre that sometimes threatened to become derivative, still had plenty of life in it on the C64. It's really the visual presentation of this game more than anything that leaps out at you. It looks amazing and the surreal nature of the characters and plot merely adds to the appeal. Thankfully, Wizball not only looks great but plays great too and the attractive graphics are not merely a misleading lid for shallow gameplay. This game was highly acclaimed upon release and earned 96% in ZZAP!64 - meaning it feel just short of a prestigious Gold Medal award.

This is a different and rather imaginative take on the scrolling shooter game. It has a great control system and the story and world it takes part in is quite charming. It has great music - by Martin Galway, and charming, surreal graphics. One nice aspect is the look of the grey worlds as they become coloured. The sound effects are very atmospheric. The game is quite challenging but highly addictive. The game was lauded for taking full advantage of the C64 hardware. This was made by Sensible Software - who also created games such as Parallax, Shoot-'Em-Up Construction Kit and Sensible Soccer. Wizball is terrific stuff and one of the most memorable of the gazillions of shooters which flooded the C64 in the mid 80s.

As for other shoot em ups on the C64, well, that is a book in itself. There are millions of them. What are the best ones that we've yet to mention in this book? The 1988 Imagine game Salamander is a lot of fun and gives you plenty of arcade style action with bright graphics, great weapon effects, swirling constantly attacking enemies, and a jaunty soundtrack that drives the action but might possibly become annoying in the end! You've seen it all before but Salamander does it it very well. Another game worth playing is the 1987 Thalamus release Hunter's Moon. This game is beautifully presented with great graphics and colour and feels like a slightly novel spin on the usual shoot em up fare in that you can travel in any direction and even engage in some exploration. The shooting action itself is very satisfying though.

An oldie but a goodie when it comes to C64 shoot em ups is the 1984 Activision game River Raid. This game looks downright primitive today but it is fast and fun to play. The gameplay in River Raid is pretty timeless and was borrowed by numerous other games but the original is still worth a look. We can't discuss C64 shoot em ups without mentioning 1942 - a World War 2 arcade conversion that literally everyone who owned a C64 must have played at some point. 1942 isn't tremendously well regarded on the C64 but I remember playing this to death and having some fun with it. The music in 1942 will rattle around in your head for days afterwards.

The 1986 C64 conversion of the arcade shoot em up Nemesis is definitely well polished and fun and worth a look. Though you might feel like you've seen this sort of game a million times before Nemesis has some enjoyable backdrops and obstacles to mitigate the deja vu. The 1989 Rainbow Arts shooter X-Out is excellent too and one of the best games of its type on the C64. The weapons and boss battles make X-Out fun - even if it isn't exactly the most original game in the world. Bandits is a 1983 shooter by Sirius Software that is basically a slightly souped up Space Invaders. Bandits is quite well regarded and fun for a while although it may have limited playability in the long run.

Terra Cresta is a vertical shoot em up published by Imagine in 1985. This game was yet another arcade conversion. Though the reviews were quite sniffy in places (I'm looking at you ZZAP!64), Terra Cresta is a perfectly competent and playable shooter which I can remember owning and enjoying. The 1984 Activision shooter Zone Ranger is not bad. This game is sort of like Asteroids crossed with Dropzone and has you in control of a ship that has to blast satellites. The novelty here is that you sometimes end up in the sanctuary of a maze. The graphics in

Zone Ranger are somewhat dated compared to slicker (and later C64 shooters) but the game is entertaining enough.

The 1984 Activision game Pastfinder is another oldie but goodie. This game is sort of like River Raid but with a sci-fi twist. The graphics are understandably a little rough around the edges compared to later C64 shooters but there is plenty of colour in the backdrops and the gameplay is pretty good. The 1989 game Silk Worm is worth a look if you like blasting action. This game is a horizontally scrolling shooter and yet another arcade conversion. This game is quite novel in that the player can alternate between controlling a helicopter or a jeep. The game is pretty frenetic (which is obviously a good thing) and has some nice backdrops and colours. The scrolling is smooth and impressive too.

The 1986 Ocean game Parallax is worth a mention in any discussion of C64 shoot em ups. This game looks a bit like Uridium but has some interesting gameplay mechanics in that you have to get out of the ship you are piloting and walk around to complete missions. It's almost like a shoot em up with arcade adventure elements. SWIV is a 1991 vertically scrolling shoot em up that plays like a souped up more modern 1942. It's perfectly competent and enjoyable for what it is and worth a look. By the way, in case you were wondering, SWIV stands for Special Weapons Interdiction Vehicle. You learn something new every day!

The 1986 Thalamus game Sanxion is a pretty well regarded C64 shooter and managed to earn sizzler status in ZZAP!64 with 93%. Sanxion is a horizontally-scrolling shooter where you race across the screen blasting everything. Sanxion is quite interesting in that it has a split-screen design with the smaller portion of the top of the screen offering a top down view of the action. While a nice gimmick it doesn't feel completely necessary. That aside though Sanxion is good stuff. The scrolling is smooth, the game is fast, and there are some enjoyably trippy colours and flourishes. It's a pretty tough game too so Sanxion will certainly test your mettle.

I gave Falcon Patrol a mention in the introduction to this book so I might as well give it another mention now. It's a very early side scrolling shooter and good retro fun. Falcon Patrol II (which is essentially more of the same but slightly improved) is also a lot of fun. Two other shooters worth playing are Crazy Comets and its sequel Mega Apocalypse. These games were released by Martech. If you need yet more colourful blasting action then these two games are pretty good. There are literally hundreds of decent shooters we haven't got around to mentioning on the C64. If you do some investigating you should be able to find many more gems.

WHO DARES WINS II (1985)

Label: Alligata, Designer: Steve Evans

Who Dares Wins II is a top down shoot em up game. The player controls a soldier who is sent into an enemy area. He is armed with a gun and grenades and must capture enemy outposts and rescue prisoners. Who Dares Wins II is a very entertaining shoot em up. It is basically a cheeky rip-off of Commando - the arcade game which was converted to home computers (including the C64). The game was first released as Who Dares Wins but the makers (Elite) of the C64 version of Commando gained an injunction to stop the game being sold. Alligata then changed the game slightly and released it as Who Dares Wins II. This is actually better than the C64 version of Commando. It has great variety in the levels and the controls are good - enabling the player to throw grenades and fire in all directions easily.

There is a good range of vehicles and planes in the game too. It is very satisfying in this game to get to the end of a level and see what the next screen is and so Who Dares Wins II is very addictive. This is a terrific little game and great fun for anyone who enjoyed Commando. It's basically like an unlicenced version of Commando! The only downside to the game is the loop of Colonel Bogey on the soundtrack. This might get on your nerves after a while! There are few games I played more on the C64 than Who Dares Wins II. It might look primitive to modern eyes but in 1985 this game was pretty amazing and gave C64 users many happy hours of fun. By the way, I love the action Man style art on the box for this game.

On the subject of Who Dares Wins II, what about the actual licenced version of Commando that was released on the C64 by elite in 1985? Well, this game is pretty good fun and has a fantastic soundtrack. For some reason though I always found it less playable than Who Dares Wins II - which is strange as they are more or less the same game. I think it has something to do with the fact that in Who Dares Wins II the gameplay is slightly slower and more measured so this means the controls feel easier. Another thing is that in Who Dares Wins II it's more satisfying when you shoot people or blow things up. This might have someting to do with the fact that Who Dares Wins II has larger and blockier graphics than Commando but it's also obviously a consequence of the respective sound effects more than anything. You should still play Commando but, personally, I just always preferred Who Dares Wins II. One major disappointment with Commando too was that it only had three of the arcade version's eight levels.

As far as Commando clones go, one of the best ones on the C64 was Ikari Warriors - which was released by Elite in 1988 and based on an arcade machine. This is a Rambo inspired game (I gather it was originally intended to be a licenced Rambo game but they obviously didn't obtain the rights in the end) in which you move through the jungtle killing hordes of soldiers and blowing up tanks and helicopters. The graphics are a trifle dated even for 1988 but they do the job and the ever changing jungle backdrops are fun with rivers and bridges. It's fun too how you can hop in a tank for extra firepower and there's a two-player mode also. Ikari Warriors is a lot of fun and worth playing. It's quite challenging too so you'll feel a sense of achievement if you beat it.

As for licenced Rambo games, there was a Rambo: First Blood Part II game released by Ocean in 1986. The game is basically another Commando clone. The music is excellent but the actual graphics and gameplay in Rambo leave something to be desired. I can remember playing this and enjoying at first the fact that you have more freedom to explore than other Commando clones and also liking the way you can blow up the environment around you but I got bored of the actual game pretty fast. Rambo: First Blood Part II is worth a look but don't expect anything too amazing.

As far as top down Commando-ish games go, one of the very best ones is the 1988 game Alien Syndrome. This is a conversion of a famous arcade machine. The game (which is clearly inspired by the Alien franchise) and has you as an all action exterminator investigating a colony festooned with aliens. Alien Syndrome is sort of like a mix of Commando, Gauntlet, and an Aliens game and has plenty of atmosphere and pleasantly crisp graphics. The aliens are nicely colourful and detailed in the game and the backdrops are pretty good too. You even get a few boss fights. Alien Syndrome is sort of like a top down version of Doom and very entertaining on the whole.

One of my favourite Commando clones is a game called L.A. SWAT - which was released by Mastertronic in 1986. This game was one of my C64 guilty pleasures. L.A. SWAT is a top down shoot em up which scrolls up vertically. The player is policeman in Los Angeles battling rioters. The policeman moves up the street shooting rioters who are armed with petrol bombs and clubs. At the end of each level a gang member moves around holding a woman hostage and must be shot. There are rooftop snipers opposing you. The levels get harder with more gang members and roadblocks. Senior citizens are also present- with points are deducted if they are accidentally shot.

A slightly bad taste game (though the controversy seems tame from a modern vantage point where many games are very violent!) but an extremely enjoyable one, L.A. SWAT is a lot of fun and a fairly mindless but diverting shooter which does more or less all you ask of it. While you wouldn't say this was a classic game I had a great time blasting my way through this. It is similar to games like Commando and Who Dares Wins II but in an urban setting with the police. The graphics are ok and the music is a bit monotone but suits the style of the game. And the game was a budget title on release too so it can be forgiven for being slightly unpolished. The game is very addictive and good undemanding budget fun. L.A. SWAT is a simple game and just very enjoyable as you shoot all the gang members.

Another guilty pleasure of mine on the C64 is the equally violent Death Wish 3. This 1986 game by Gremlin is based on the Charles Bronson film. You are the vigilante Paul Kersey and must run around New York shooting violent criminals. This game is a side scroller and nothing amazing graphically but the gameplay is fun and rather gruesome too. When you shoot someone with a rocket launcher they dissolve into a puddle of bloody gibs. This might have been the first time I'd seen gibbbing in a computer game and it was sort of fun to see gore and violence like this in a C64 game. L.A. SWAT and Death Wish 3 are hardly great games but I found both of them to be both fun to play and amusing. If you want to see some very early examples of violent shooters then both of these games offer some good old fashioned undemanding fun. They don't have the enduring playability of more classic games but you'll probably have got your money's worth by the time you are done.

By the way, if you are looking for a new twist on the top down shooter type of games you should play the 1987 MicroProse Software game Airbourne Ranger. Airborne Ranger is an action game. The player us a US Army Ranger who is undertaking several missions. These include destroying a bunker, rescuing a POW and capturing an enemy officer. The player has a plan of the mission at the start and chooses a Ranger from a selection available. Firstly the player drops ammo over the enemy area via a plane, which will be used during the mission. Then the Ranger is parachuted into the area and must complete the mission contending with enemy soldiers in foxholes and bunkers and mine fields. Once the mission is completed the Ranger has to go to a puck up point. A successful mission means promotion.

Airborne Ranger is a great action game. It is similar to ordinary top down shoot em ups such as Commando and Who Dares wins II but with a different perspective and more in depth with an added strategy element. One good thing about the game is that for each mission a random map is generated. There is a lot of variety in the gameplay and different ways to use stealth to complete the mission. The AI is good too. The sound effects - such as the enemy soldier's footsteps are very atmospheric. Airbourne Ranger is good stuff on the whole.

WORLD GAMES (1986)

Label: Epyx, Designer: Numerous

This is the fourth entry in Epyx's iconic Games series after Summer Games (1984) Summer Games II (1985) and Winter Games (1986). There are a nice selection of sports in the game. All the different sports have good controls which means they can be played again and again. All are fun – sometimes these multi-sports games have a few duffers but the Epyx games managed to avoid this pitfall. This one has some less traditional sports such as barrel jumping and caber toss. Weightlifting and slalom skiing, which both feature here, would have been at home in the first three Epyx collections of traditional sports games. The presentation is very slick as usual. The graphics are up to the usual high standards of the Epyx sports games and they were getting better with each entry.

Up to eight players can compete in World Games. Gold, silver and bronze medal are awarded for each event. Records can be saved. In World Games the characters seem bigger than previous Epyx sports games which is a plus. In this game there are also travelogues giving some detail on the history of each event. There are lots of amusing animations and the snippets of humour increase the enjoyment. There is a great soundtrack to the game with different music for each event. Apparently football (soccer) was going to be included as the German event instead of barrel jumping but it would have been too complex to include a whole football sim.

A penalty shoot-out game was considered before barrel jumping was chosen. The full list of sports in the game are - Weightlifting (Russia), Barrel Jumping (Germany), Cliff Diving (Mexico), Slalom Skiing (France), Log Rolling (Canada), Bull Riding (USA), Caber Toss (Scotland), Sumo Wrestling (Japan). The cliff diving is fantastic - there is just something very satisfying about executing a great dive and then landing in that little rock pool with the pelican perched above you. The slalom skiing definitely feels like a leftover idea from Winter Games but it's pretty good.

The only event here which is arguably weaker is the log rolling. The log rolling feels a trifle too silly and comical for an Epyx game and it isn't that interesting relative to the other events. It's great by the way to get a combat sim at the end with the sumo wrestling. This is wonderfully animated and great fun. One might have expected this series to have run its course after three previous games but World Games showed there was still life left in the Epyx multi-sports concept. This is a very classy and enjoyable addition to the Epyx sports library and another C64 classic. The cover art for this was amazing too.

By the way, a parody of this game - titled Alternative World Games - was released by Gremlin in 1987. Alternative World Games has events like pogo stick, pillow fight, and boot throwing. The game is decent fun with cartoonish graphics. The backdrops are pretty good - especially a gondola scene in

Venice. Alternative World Games is nothing earth shattering but an amusingly affectionate parody of the Epyx games that should provide some undemanding fun. The game was actually good enough to get 86% in ZZAP!64. There were numerous other variants or parodies of the Epyx sports series. We've already covered the best ones so what is left? Well, many of them were awful but Knight Games, Western Games, and Pub Games were modest fun for a few plays and might be worth checking out.

ZAC MCKRACKEN AND THE ALIEN MINDBENDERS (1988)

Label: Lucasfilm Games, Designer: David Fox

Zak McKracken and the Alien Mindbenders is one of the early Lucasfilm adventure games and in the vein of later classics like Monkey Island. This is one of the most ambitious games ever made for the C64 and remains very cultish and popular. The plot has a writer named Zak (Francis Zachary McKracken) attempting to stop aliens from reducing the intelligence of people on earth. If you've enjoyed some of the other Lucasfilm games you'll know what to expect here. You get adventure, humour, many jokes, a lot of puzzles, and globe-trotting fun with plenty of invention and charm.

These sorts of games can be an acquired taste (I know people who hate Monkey Island style adventures because they always get stuck early on!) but if you are a fan of them you should have a lot of fun with Zak McKracken and the Alien Mindbenders. This game is very long by C64 standards (and was only available on disk at the time) so great value for money and is full of inventive set-pieces. More than anything these types of games give the player a memorable gaming experience. You really feel like you've been on an adventure yourself after playing one of the Lucasfilm games for a long period.

The graphics are (obviously) not quite as polished as the games Lucasfilm would release in the years to come but very good for the time with plenty of colour and charm. Such is the cultish longevity of this game that fans have produced a number of unofficial sequels and remakes. The original is still well worth playing though. Zak McKracken and the Alien Mindbenders is a remarkably inventive and engaging adventure game that may be the best of its type ever produced for the C64. The graphics and backdrops are excellent and the various characters are all nicely conveyed. The sci-fi flourishes in this game are terrific too when they arrive.

One of the great pleasures of Zak McKracken and the Alien Mindbenders is making progress in the game and enjoying all the various backdrops and locations as you get further and further into your adventure. This makes the game a very rewarding experience and motivates the player to keep going deeper and deeper into the game. Despite the fact that the graphics seem rather dated today Zak McKracken and the Alien Mindbenders is one of the best adventure games ever created and fully deserving of its lofty status as one of the classics of the C64.